One-Room Schools
of the Middle West

One-Room

WAYNE E. FULLER

Schools of the Middle West

AN ILLUSTRATED HISTORY

University Press of Kansas

Published by the University Press of Kansas (Lawrence,
Kansas 66049), which was organized by the Kansas Board of
Regents and is operated and funded by Emporia State Uni-
versity, Fort Hays State University, Kansas State University,
Pittsburg State University, the University of Kansas, and
Wichita State University

Library of Congress Cataloging-in-Publication Data

Fuller, Wayne Edison, 1919–
    One-room schools of the Middle West: an illustrated
history / Wayne E. Fuller
    p. cm.
    ISBN 0-7006-0637-8 (cloth)
1. Rural schools—Middle West—History. 2. Rural schools—
Middle West—History—Pictorial works. 1. Title
LB1564.F85 1994
370.19'346'0977—dc20   94-15799

British Library Cataloguing in Publication Data is available.

Printed in the United States of America

10 9 8 7 6 5 4 3 2 1

The paper used in this publication meets the minimum
requirements of the American National Standard for Perma-
nence of Paper for Printed Library Materials z39.48-1984.

Book design by Kathleen Szawiola

*To Kimberly and Amanda, who
will never know the trials or
triumphs of attending a
one-room school, and to all
those who do*

Contents

Abbreviations

FERA	Federal Emergency Relief Administration
FSA	Farm Security Administration
GCMHS	Goodhue County, Minnesota, Historical Society
GPO	Government Printing Office
KSHS	Kansas State Historical Society
LC	Library of Congress
MHS	Minnesota Historical Society
MSHS	Missouri State Historical Society
NA	National Archives
NSHS	Nebraska State Historical Society
OHS	Ohio Historical Society
SHSI	State Historical Society of Iowa
SHSW	State Historical Society of Wisconsin
TCHA	Tippecanoe County Historical Association

Preface

The Country Schoolhouse

The little country schoolhouse—you
Remember it; of course you do.
Within the angle snugly set,
Where two long yellow highways met,
And saplings planted here and there
About the yard and boxed with care
As if to typify, in turn,
The youngsters caught and caged, to learn.

Around, the rolling pastures spread
With woodland patches garlanded,
From which the breezes gladly bore
Sly invitations to the door.
Across the sills the bees' soft hum
Was mingled with the muttered sum,
And from their cover in the vale
In plaintive pleading the quail.

With basket and with pail equipped,
Clear-eyes, tan cheeked and berry-lipped,
Athwart the pasture, down the road,
They trudged to learning's poor abode;
The pink sunbonnet, broad-brimmed straw;
The bare brown feet that knew no law

Of fashion's last; the bundled forms
That laughed aloud at cold and storms.

What tales the scarred desks might relate
Of triumph gained from book and slate;
What lore the clapboards loose possess,
Of feat at noontime and recess!
And doomed how oft the panes to see,
Back up the road and o'er the lea,
Haste boy and girl, new worlds to find,
The little schoolhouse left behind.

O little country school! In vain
May critics hold you in disdain.
The greatest lessons that you taught
Were not by chalk and pencil wrought,
As op'd your door on fields and sky,
So, likewise just as wide and high,
You opened to the eyes of youth
The principles of love and truth.

—Edwin Sabin, "The Country
Schoolhouse" (State Historical
Society of Iowa, Iowa City,
Agnes Samuelson Manuscripts)

P.1. The one-room school, like the log cabin, evoked images of the nation's rural roots—the source of its strength—and became a useful symbol for all things American. Attacked for their attempted regulation of parochial schools during the election of 1890, Wisconsin Republicans used the one-room schoolhouse to illumine their defense of public education. (Whi [X3] 21952, SHSW)

When midwesterner Edwin Sabin wrote "The Country Schoolhouse" in 1909, thousands of one-room schoolhouses still dotted the Middle West. Yet the poem, like John Greenleaf Whittier's "Schoolhouse," written nearly fifty years before, evoked such wistful memories and haunting scenes that it left the impression that the little schools had vanished with the frontier.

We will never know exactly what inspired these men to write so nostalgically of one-room schools even before their time had passed. Perhaps it was that the schools brought back memories of their own childhoods, when they had trudged to school along dusty country roads and triumphed there with book and slate. Or possibly they saw in those unpretentious frame buildings monuments to their parents' struggles and aspirations to educate them in the face of so much hardship. More likely, they remembered their little schools so fondly because it was there that they met their friends, played games, competed with one another, and found a diversion from the lonely life on the farm. Sabin's poem, however, could well have been his way of defending the one-room school from the harsh attacks being made on it in the early 1900s.

Whatever their inspiration, these poems and reminiscences of attending the Midwest's one-room schools were unique. White students in no other school in the American experience, least of all those in large urban schools with their bleak brick exteriors and treeless asphalt playgrounds, ever portrayed their school days as lovingly.

Like the log cabin, the small school's image evoked unforgettable sentiments that made it useful to politician, patriot, and poet alike. In 1890, when a major conflict erupted in Wisconsin over the Republican-dominated legislature's attempt to control parochial schools, the Republicans used the one-room school to defend themselves and public schools. Suddenly pictures of "The Little Schoolhouse," with captions urging voters to "stand by it," were everywhere and even wound up on Republican stationery. [Illus. P.1] Six years later it figured prominently in the heated presidential race between William McKinley and William Jennings Bryan. Posing as the "home defenders" in its campaign poster, the Republican party conveyed the impression that it would defend not only the nation's farms and industry with a protective tariff but also the little red schoolhouse, symbol of the nation's glorious effort to educate all its people. [Illus. P.2]

That symbol would be made to carry even greater weight. In 1897, an artist wrapped an

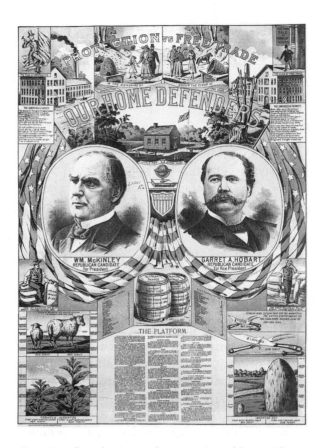

P.2. *In the election of 1896, Republican "home defenders" promised that the protective tariff would save the nation's farms and factories and even the education, patriotism, and morality symbolized by the "little red schoolhouse." (LC)*

P.3. *Wrapped in the flag, the one-room school was the symbol for the nation's devotion to education, democracy, patriotism, and morality. (LC)*

P.4. *Failure to teach children traditional values in today's schools is poignantly illustrated by an artist's sketch of students drifting away from the one-room schoolhouse. (Christopher Bing,* Christian Science Monitor, *Jan. 30, 1987, p. B12)*

early American flag around the little school and labeled it "Standards of America," invoking images of the American zeal for education, democracy, morality, and presumably every other noble American trait. [Illus. P.3]

The one-room school has become so deeply embedded in the American consciousness that today, long after most such schools have disappeared, it is still a useful symbol. Etched on the cover of a magazine or headlining a newspaper story on education, with flag flying and belfry reaching to the sky, it remains the nation's most enduring symbol of education and the traditional values it once embraced.

In the January 30, 1987, issue of the *Christian Science Monitor* appeared a story lamenting the teaching in today's schools that all values are equally valid and, and in effect, demeaning tradi-

tional western values of right and wrong. Fittingly, the sketch headlining the article asked if "values neutrality" had "left students adrift" and depicted children in rowboats drifting away from a sinking one-room school! [Illus. P.4]

As they sift through stories of the crisis in education that now engulfs the nation, few Americans are likely to wonder about the history of the one-room school that evokes such powerful images. Country schools seem so remote, and the perplexities that plague our large urban schools are so massive, it scarcely seems possible that the one-room school experience has any relevance today. Yet Americans who are concerned about the awesome problems schools face in their attempt to educate today's children may find instructive the story of how former generations of Americans, acting almost alone and with the barest of resources, overcame the obstacles to educating their children. The story of how they did that is told here in words and in pictures—how plain midwestern farmers organized and maintained one-room schools that virtually wiped out illiteracy, strengthened their children's devotion to democracy, gave them a taste of the world's best literature, and taught them right from wrong along the way.

To be sure, this might have been easier to do in simpler times, when the hurdles were not so overwhelming. But who is to say that the problems those midwestern farmers confronted were any less formidable for them than the problems their urban descendants face today? Perhaps the one-room schools were able to achieve so much not because they had so few problems to overcome but because they were never abandoned by those whose interests they served. Controlled in nearly every detail by the parents of the children who attended them, one-room schools were the centers of community life; they were so small that no student was unimportant. The little one-room schools of the Middle West offer important lessons in education, even in our own times of sophisticated educational theory and large, professionally dominated schools.

The images that appear in this volume were collected over more than twenty years. During that time, it was my pleasure to meet many helpful archivists in the iconographic sections of all the midwestern state historical societies (except for those of North and South Dakota), in county and university archives, in the Library of Congress, and in the Lilly Library at Indiana University. Many of the photographs used here are from their collections. Regrettably, they are too numerous to mention by name, but I thank them for their ready responses to my inquiries.

I am also grateful for the support given to this project by the research institute at the University of Texas at El Paso.

I am especially indebted to Walter M. Anderson of Emporia, Kansas, who gave me access to his private collection of Kansas school scenes, and to Odessa Ofstad, curator of the special collection at Northeast Missouri State University, who found some of the photographs of the Porter School for me.

Many of the photographs were copied from bulletins of the Bureau of Education and other government publications; from the school records of Kansas, Nebraska, Wisconsin, and Michigan; and from magazines and newspapers. Dan Miller, head of the Media Center at the University of Texas at El Paso—himself a graduate of a one-room school—photographed these for me. I am particularly grateful not only for his willingness to go beyond routine to obtain the best possible reproductions but also for his unfailing courtesy.

Finally, thanks to my wife, Billie, who patiently toured the rural Midwest with me, helped find old country schools from nineteenth-century plats, read the manuscript, and reminded me from time to time that there was more work to be done. I owe much to her for the completion of the manuscript and to my daughter, Jamie, who spent a Christmas vacation reading it and finding errors that I had been confident were not there.

One-Room Schools
of the Middle West

Chapter

I

Democracy in Small Places

From beginning to end, the Midwest was always the special home of one-room schoolhouses. From Ohio west to Kansas and Nebraska, and from Minnesota and North Dakota south to Missouri, more than 90,000 one-room schoolhouses—almost as many as in the rest of the nation combined—cast their small shadows across country schoolyards as late as 1918. In comparison, that year there were about 62,000 one-room schoolhouses in the South, 24,500 in the Northeast, and 15,000 in the West (U.S. Bureau of Education, Bulletin no. 90 [Washington, D.C.: GPO, 1921], pp. 165–66). To this day, thousands of midwesterners whose memories stretch from World War I to the Depression to World War II can still remember their days in one-room schools.

Education was the Midwest's birthright. In words that echoed through the years, it was conferred upon the region by the same law that established government there in 1787. "Religion, morality, and knowledge," read the famous Ordinance of 1787, "being necessary to good government, and the happiness of mankind, schools and the means of education shall forever be preserved."

1.1. The Land Ordinance of 1785 provided that government land be divided into townships and sections, with section sixteen of every township set aside to support education. Money derived from this source became the nucleus of an educational fund in midwestern states.

6	.5	4	3	2	1
7	8	9	10	11	12
18	17	✕	15	14	13
19	20	21	22	23	24
30	29	28	27	26	25
31	32	33	34	35	36

TOWNSHIP AND SECTIONS--SCHOOL SECTION 16

and morality could preserve order and create the virtuous republic they had set their hearts on.

Their concern for education in the region had really surfaced two years earlier, when, confronted by the need to measure government land for sale in that vast garden beyond the Appalachians, they enacted the Ordinance of 1785. This law provided for surveys that eventually divided the land into ranges, townships, and sections. Range lines ran north and south; within the ranges, townships six miles square were paced off. Townships were divided into thirty-six sections, each containing 640 acres. These were numbered one to thirty-six, always beginning, after 1796, at the northeast corner of the township and moving to the left.

Section sixteen of every township was set aside for education. In years to come, the revenue from these sections, mismanaged and abused though it was, formed the nucleus of an educational fund that allowed each midwestern state to start creating a system of free public education. [Illus. 1.1] The Ordinance of 1785 did more. It shaped the face of our country, giving it that square configuration we see as we fly over it. Beyond that, it simplified the division of the land into well-defined units that served purposes its authors could not have imagined in 1785.

Following the surveys into western lands, settlers created counties—such as Rock County, Wisconsin—named the townships they settled in, and established governments in both. [Illus. 1.2] In time, they established farms within their townships—sometimes covering an entire section, but more often only a half, a quarter, or even an eighth of a section. The survey system made it possible for every farm, whether large or small, to have a precise location, as did every other important site in the township: churches, roads, cemeteries, schools, and even, beginning in the twentieth century, rural mail routes. Over the years, most of these appeared on interesting county maps that still tell us much about midwestern rural life in the nineteenth century. [Illus. 1.3]

The survey system also gave farmers the exact mechanism they needed to lay out the boundaries of small, independent school districts, such as that of District No. 37, Ross Township, Osborne

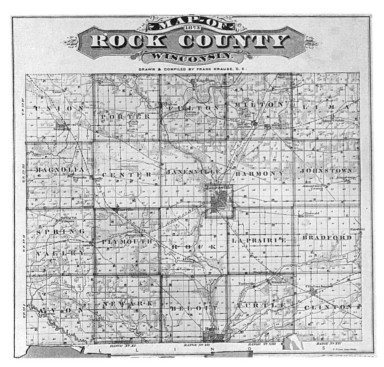

1.2. Settlers followed the surveys into fertile lands, created counties and townships, gave them names, and established governments in both. (New Combination Atlas of Rock County, Wisconsin, 1873 [Chicago, 1873], p. 5)

If this prescription for good government sounds simplistic and even quaint two hundred years later, it was only common sense to the men of the Revolution. They had just established a republic that was loosely knit under the Articles of Confederation and encircled by monarchies; they knew that where there is no king, all men are kings. Wise in the ways of the world, they also knew that only education linked to religion

1.3. The survey system made it possible to map the precise locations of farms, churches, cemeteries, and schoolhouses and the boundaries of small, independent school districts. (Plat Book of Dodge County, Wisconsin [Minneapolis, 1890], p. 44)

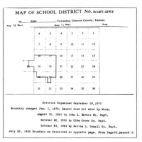

1.4. The Midwest was carved into thousands of small school districts like that of District No. 37, Osborne County, Kansas. (School Records, KSHS)

1.5. Notices were posted around the district summoning farmers to the annual school meeting. (Dist. No. 37, Osborne Co., Kans., School Records, KSHS)

County, Kansas. Its boundary, established in 1873, had been changed four times by 1925 when, according to the description, it began, "at the N.E. corner of the S.E. 1/4 of Section 17," ran "west 2 miles to the N.W. corner of S.W. 1/4 of Section 18, thence south 1/2 mile, to the S.W. corner of Section 18, thence west 1/2 mile, thence south 1/2 mile," and so on until it reached the place where it had begun. [Illus. 1.4]

As the years passed, the Midwest was carved into thousands of such patches of earth, each with its own schoolhouse, community life, and history. Individualistic, democratic, and often contentious, the little independent school districts were among the most important institutions in the rural Midwest. Yet their importance to rural life has gone largely unnoticed, for obvious reasons. Originating in New England and carried across the Appalachians by its sons and daughters, the school districts were so small and so common that it was easy to take them for granted and overlook the remarkable ways farmers used them to order their society.

Usually no larger than six or seven sections, each school district contained as many as thirty families or as few as twelve—perhaps fewer. No two were shaped exactly alike, but most had at least one thing in common: State laws had made the school districts corporations, and the farmers who lived in them were the stockholders, with almost unlimited authority. Once each year, and sometimes more often, notices were posted around the district, summoning farmers for a school meeting. There they would gather to provide the necessities for the coming school year. Sometimes only a handful came; on other occasions, so many showed up that the little schoolroom could barely hold them all. Whatever the number, in those small places, the meeting quickly became an exercise in democracy. [Illus. 1.5]

Imagine a musty schoolroom, perhaps no more than twenty-two by eighteen feet in size. It is a hot summer day, and the three windows on each side of the little building have been opened to whatever breeze the afternoon or evening air might provide. The chairman is seated at the teacher's desk, overlooking seven, eight, or even a dozen or more farmers scattered about the room, seated at their children's desks. As the first order of business, he calls for the approval of the minutes of the last meeting, or perhaps the treasurer's report, and then turns to setting the length of the winter and spring school terms.

When that is accomplished, the meeting moves on to other school affairs. Passing motion after

1.6. District clerks recorded the minutes of school meetings, leaving to posterity the job of ferreting out the history of their schools. (Jt. Dist. No. 7, East Troy and Waterford Twps., Walworth and Racine Cos., Wis., School Records, SHSW)

1.8. School board elections, which were often hotly contested, removed some board members and elevated others to office. (Fractional Dist. No. 1, Tecumseh Twp., Lenawee Co., Mich., School Records, Mich. Historical Collections, Bentley Historical Library, Univ. of Mich.)

motion, the farmers instruct the school board on what kind of teacher to employ, even going so far in some instances as to exclude those of a certain religion. They determine the amount of money they will raise for the school year and provide for the year's supply of fuel. Finally, they come to the election of one member of the three-member school board. When they finish, the clerk records

1.7. The farmers learned parliamentary procedure from instructions given in Welch's Teachers' Classification Register. *(Jt. Dist. No. 2, Albion and Sumner Twps., Dane Co., Wis., School Records, SHSW)*

the minutes of the meeting, leaving it to posterity to ferret out the history of their schools. [Illus. 1.6]

How did these largely uneducated and unsophisticated farmers know the parliamentary procedures they used to conduct their meetings in such an orderly fashion? For the uninitiated, a page of instructions from the district record book offered a guide, but older leaders rarely had to use it. [Illus. 1.7] Over the years, the mechanisms of democracy became almost second nature to them. Most learned nearly all of what they knew about debating, making and rescinding motions, and even Latin phrases such as sine die in those same district meetings, which were, in fact, democracy's training ground. Just as the small, independent school districts were the smallest self-governing units in the nation, so their school meetings were the nearest thing the nation had to pure democracy (except for New England town meetings).

At these often disputatious and protracted meetings, both native and foreign-born Americans learned to participate in making decisions and took their first lessons in politics. Sides were taken and debated; arguments were won and lost. Elections, often hotly contested, removed some from office and elevated others to places of responsibility on the school board. [Illus. 1.8]

Because so few people lived in each school district, nearly every farmer there, no matter how unprepared, had a chance to be elected to the school board. The result was that many whose qualities seemed rather undistinguished discovered talents they never knew they possessed and

1.9. The district treasurer's report reveals much about the operation and maintenance of a one-room school. (Dist. No. 3, Montrose Twp., Dane Co., Wis., School Records, SHSW)

1.10. School board members devoted many hours to buying supplies, repairing the school well, and fixing leaky stovepipes. (SHSM)

became community leaders through their work on the school board. Trained for leadership in this cradle of democracy, more than one such farmer eventually entered a larger political arena.

Those school boards did for their country schools what professional bureaucrats—superintendents, principals, counselors, and supervisors—do for our large urban schools today. They were the farmers' executive officers; they presided at school meetings, employed teachers, reported the number of children in their schools to the county superintendent, and recorded the minutes of every school meeting. They purchased all their schools' supplies and paid the bills.

The annual treasurer's report, often laboriously prepared on the kitchen table, told the farmers, as it tells us, much about school finances and operation. [Illus. 1.9] The simplicity of the treasurer's report can be misleading, however. Only by reading between the lines can we appreciate the time the board members must have spent employing someone to clean and whitewash the schoolhouse, repair the stovepipe, fix the well, buy supplies, and perform a long list of other chores. [Illus. 1.10]

To be sure, the treasurer's reports were as inelegant as the little schoolhouse. The clerks' reports summing up the number of students and other details were sometimes woefully incomplete. Smooth-talking salesmen occasionally beguiled the school board into purchasing nearly worthless learning charts. But even if some of the board members were incompetent, interested principally in self-promotion, or serving only to prevent higher taxes (as was sometimes alleged), there was no doubt that the vast majority, working for little or nothing, did what they did because they were interested in the education of

their children and in the welfare of the little community that gave meaning to their lives.

The well-known historian Richard Hofstadter once suggested that American farmers had no communities worthy of the name; he contended that they were too isolated, too individualistic, and too anxious to sell out and make a profit to build communities. But the history of those diminutive independent school districts reveals how little this observation applied to the reality of midwestern rural life. Advancing into forestlands and plains where no settled communities had ever been, midwestern farmers used their small school districts as the cornerstones of community life as well as instruments for educating their children and practicing democracy.

The district's boundaries determined the extent of their community, identified their location in the county, gave them a sense of belonging to a place, and, in the end, forced community responsibilities upon them that they would not otherwise have had. The schoolhouse was the community center and often the only public building in the district. On Sunday, it was the church; on election day, it was the polling place. At other times, it was a theater, where dramas and debates were held; a lodge for Grange meetings; and a forum for politicians. In the early 1900s, it was even a model for urbanites who were attempting to build community centers in the middle of their disorderly cities.

One has only to listen to the nostalgic song of the Social Center Association of America, an ambitious organization designed to promote urban community spirit in the years before the First World War, to see how these urbanites perceived the role of the country school in rural communities:

Come close and let us wake the joy
Our fathers used to know
When to the little schoolhouse
Together they would go.
Then neighbor's heart to neighbor warmed
In thought for common good;
We'll strike the fine old chord again—
A song of neighborhood.

Whether farmers really thought philosophically of their schoolhouses as community builders is open to question. What midwestern settlers did know was that they had to have schools for their children, and they rushed to build them almost as soon as they built their homes.

Chapter

2

Pioneer Schools

2.1. *The first places of learning in the pioneer Midwest were log schoolhouses. Constructed without nails or anything made of iron, some stood for years. This was the first log schoolhouse in Adams County, Indiana.* (Twenty-eighth Biennial Report of the Superintendent of Public Instruction, Indiana [Fort Wayne, Ind., 1917], opp. p. 201)

Frederick Jackson Turner, the great historian of the American West, had many things right. As he saw it, for nearly three hundred years the history of the United States was partly the story of beginning again. "American social development," he wrote in 1893, "has been continually beginning over again on the frontier." As long as empty spaces stretched across the hinterland, thousands of Americans left the settled portion of the country to return, as Turner wrote, "to primitive conditions on a continually advancing frontier." There the settlers built anew the institutions they had left behind, but they were never quite the same. Turner never mentioned it, but the primitive schoolhouses the midwestern settlers built as they poured into what was to become the nation's heartland were excellent illustrations of his thesis.

Built in small forest clearings or on the brow of a hill, often in ill-defined districts or no districts at all, schoolhouses were among the pioneers' first community enterprises. Like their homes, the schoolhouses were made of logs—the building material at hand. No one needs to be reminded of the hardships the pioneers endured to bring civilization to the wilderness, but con-

2.2. *Clapboards attached to "weight poles" formed
the roof of primitive log schoolhouses.* (Twenty-
eighth Biennial Report of the Superintendent of Public Instruction, Indiana *[Fort Wayne, Ind., 1917]*,
opp. p. 395)

2.3. *A fireplace large enough to accommodate
six-foot logs warmed the first log schoolhouses.*
(Twenty-eighth Biennial Report of the Superintendent
of Public Instruction, Indiana *[Fort Wayne, Ind.,
1917]*, *opp. p. 395)*

sider the construction of their first public buildings. It was purely a voluntary effort. No one
could be forced to help—at least by law—and it
was always a matter of self-help. In the forest or
on the plains, there were no architects, no bureaucracy, no professional educators. Indeed,
there was little but the desire to build schoolhouses. Being resourceful people, they organized
themselves in various ways to erect their schoolhouses.

Sometimes the first school meeting consisted
of simply designating the number of logs, rafters,
or beams each farmer had to contribute to the
enterprise. When these materials were assembled,
the farmers gathered and put up the schoolhouse.
Or they might begin their work with no logs at
all, in which case they would appoint some of
the farmers to be wood choppers, some to be
haulers, others hewers, and the rest carpenters.
Organized in this fashion, they set about their
duties until the schoolhouse was raised and furnished with its crude appointments.

When completed, the schoolhouses looked
just like any other log cabins. They had no flags,
no bells, nothing to distinguish them as places of
learning. Usually they had neither nail nor any
other piece of iron holding them together. Yet so
sound was their construction that some of them
stood for years, often unoccupied, until they
became objects of veneration. Some achieved a
degree of fame as being the first schools in their
respective counties. [Illus. 2.1]

The eaves of the typical log school were about
ten feet from the ground. Its roof was made of

three-foot clapboards attached to poles (called
"weight poles") running the length of the
building—about twenty-four feet. Sturdy logs,
notched at the ends and mortised together,
formed the building's walls; mortar made from
clay soil filled the cracks between the logs. The
door was made from rough boards and hung on
leather or wooden hinges. [Illus. 2.2]

Some light was admitted into the schoolroom
through crude windows, created by cutting a slit
in one of the logs making up the wall. Occasionally one log was omitted so that the window ran
the length of the building. In either case, window
panes were made of greased paper to shed the
rain and protect against the cold.

The first log schools were heated by fireplaces.
These were constructed by cutting away some of
the logs at one end of the cabin and building a
fireplace of stone and mud in the vacant area.
Dried clay and sand were used to make the
hearth, and the chimney was fashioned out of
sticks plastered with mud. When completed, such
fireplaces were frequently large enough to accommodate six-foot logs. [Illus. 2.3] On cold
winter days, the fire roared up the big chimney,
but it rarely heated the entire room. The children
huddled as close to the open fire as possible; as
they grew warm, they shifted to permit others to
take the favored seats by the fire.

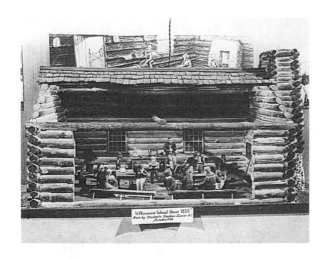

2.5. *A log schoolhouse was the setting for Edward Eggleston's description of a teacher smoking unruly students from the school. (Edward Eggleston,* The Hoosier Schoolmaster *[Bloomington: Indiana University Press/Midway Books, 1984], p. 113)*

2.4. *Backless puncheon seats and small boards attached to the walls passed for children's desks in log schoolhouses, as shown in this log school reproduction. (Whi [X3] 43027, SHSW)*

As if the cold were not enough to make young scholars uncomfortable, the schoolroom's home-made seats and writing tables tested even the most ambitious students' thirst for knowledge. The children sat on puncheon seats—log slabs that had been hewn smooth on one side and mounted on legs, but with no backs. Writing tables that passed for desks were also made of logs smoothed on one side. These were attached to the schoolhouse walls by pegs, and students who needed to write either stood up at the tables or sat in seats built high enough to reach them. [Illus. 2.4] Cheerless and uncomfortable, without pictures or adornments of any kind to relieve the bareness of the rough walls, with no maps, no blackboards, no outdoor privies, the log cabin schoolhouses were as poor as the people who built them.

This was the kind of school from which Edward Eggleston's fictional Yankee schoolmaster smoked out his unruly boys in the Flat Creek district of southern Indiana. [Illus. 2.5] Eggleston's The *Hoosier Schoolmaster* has amused thousands of readers and left them with the impression of pioneers who ridiculed "book larnin'," of teachers who taught little but spelling, and of young men whose principal aim was to force the teacher out. This impression was not entirely false. In some ways, the log schools were not unlike our contemporary schools in the untamed forests of our inner cities, where violence and illiteracy walk hand in hand.

The wonder is not that the lack of learning and discipline in Eggleston's school and in our inner-city schools is comparable. The wonder is that there was a school in Flat Creek at all. Why—in the midst of their privations and the need to build their own cabins, clear fields, plow the virgin land, plant, and harvest—did the pioneers, who presumably cared so little for education, take time to build schoolhouses? They were certainly not forced to do so. No compulsory education laws compelled them to send their children to school. There was no commission on education to set goals and no bureaucracy to sell bonds and promote the building of a schoolhouse. And except for giving land, no government—state or national—helped the pioneers build their schoolhouses in the forest. In fact, the oldest of the midwestern states, Ohio, did not even have a well-organized school system until the mid-nineteenth century. Why then?

Eggleston did not try to explain this phenomenon, which is perhaps no easier to understand than the collapse of so many of our urban schools that we were once so proud of. Then, as now, much depended on the people who lived in the community. Those pioneers who entered the Midwest from New England carried with them the tradition of public education, which they simply attempted to adapt to new circumstances. Perhaps even more important was their devout belief that children must be able to read the Bible; the ministers among them exhorted day and night that schools must be built. Indeed, the great religious revival that swept through the region with hurricane force in the 1840s contributed to

9

2.6. *In some areas, log schoolhouses were still in use long after the pioneer period had passed. This is the last log schoolhouse in Barry County, Missouri, built in 1894. (MSHS)*

2.8. *Glass windows and stove chimneys replaced greased paper panes and fireplaces in later log schoolhouses. This was the first schoolhouse in Hay Creek Township, Goodhue County, Minnesota. (GCMHS)*

the zeal to build schools in the wilderness. But neither traditions nor Bible reading could fully account for the urgency with which the pioneers erected their log schoolhouses—almost as fast as they built their own cabins. It was almost as if they feared that the dark and mysterious forest might overtake their children and reduce them to savagery if the civilizing influence of education was not immediately provided for.

Whatever the reason for their haste, the log schoolhouses scattered here and there within the

2.7. *The Michigan state superintendent found this log schoolhouse still in use in 1897 in Subdistrict No. 4, Vienna Township, Montmorency County. (Sixty-first Report of the State Superintendent of Public Instruction of the State of Michigan, 1897 [Lansing, 1898], p. 39)*

forest settlements were monuments to the pioneers' determination to educate their children. In these typical midwestern schoolhouses of the pre-Civil War era, the nation's Civil War leaders—including President Lincoln and the thousands of Northern soldiers who kept diaries and wrote their memoirs—received whatever formal education they had.

Where money was scarce and wood plentiful, farmers continued to build log schools long after the Civil War ended. As late as 1884, farmers built the last log schoolhouse in Barry County, Missouri. [Illus. 2.6] Elsewhere, log schoolhouses continued to be built in almost every midwestern state. In 1897, the state superintendent of public instruction found a log schoolhouse still in use in a lumber camp in Montmorency County, Michigan. [Illus. 2.7]

The log schoolhouses built in later years were a vast improvement over the first ones. Stoves and stovepipe chimneys replaced the big fireplaces, and glass panes replaced the greased paper windows. [Illus. 2.8] Inside, crude homemade seats and tables were pushed aside to make room for comfortable patented seats of different sizes. The little Michigan school in Subdistrict No. 4 of Vienna Township, "one of the poorest in the county," according to the state superintendent, was "warm and comfortable . . . seated with good Muskegon desks . . . and its walls . . . decorated with oak branches and paper chains

2.9. *The interior of the log school shown in Illus. 2.7 was warm and comfortable. The room had good desks and was decorated with oak branches and paper chains. (Sixty-first Report of the State Superintendent of Public Instruction of the State of Michigan, 1897 [Lansing, 1898], p. 39)*

2.10. *Outdoor privies, as well as glass windows and regular doors, were features of later log schools, such as this Minnesota schoolhouse. (Minn. State Dept. of Education)*

made by the pupils, the whole effect being cozy and cheerful." [Illus. 2.9] Finally, outdoor privies, which had not been considered necessary in more primitive times, became essential parts of the log schoolhouse landscape. [Illus. 2.10]

While the old log schoolhouses were being remodeled in the settled areas of the Middle Border, American pioneers were pushing out to homestead country on the plains of Kansas, Nebraska, and the Dakotas. And, like the earlier settlers, they began building schoolhouses to tame the raw new land as fast as they laid out their claims. In the 1870s, it was not uncommon for homesteaders to build as many as twenty schoolhouses in a county annually. But wood was so scarce there they were forced to improvise. With the same resourcefulness that marked the building of log schools in the forest clearings, the homesteaders on the plains constructed many of their schoolhouses from the sod, just as they built their homes.

One of their number described how this was done: "The site being decided upon, the neighborhood gathered with horses, plows, and wagons. A piece of virgin sod would be selected, the sod-breaking plow would be started; the sharp share would cut the grass roots and slice out a long piece of sod from two to four inches in thickness, and by twelve to fourteen inches in

width." At this point, the pieces of sod were cut into smaller segments, which became the walls of the schoolhouse. Acting as bricklayers, the farmers laid these pieces row upon row and skillfully molded them around door and window frames. Hard-to-come-by logs were then placed over the walls, and brush was thrown on the logs. Finally, sod was arranged on the brush to make a waterproof roof, and the schoolhouse was completed. [Illus. 2.11]

Not all the sod schoolhouses were constructed like houses. Some were merely dugouts, built by

2.11. *Pioneers on the plains of Kansas, Nebraska, and the Dakotas—like those in the forests—built their schoolhouses from the materials at hand. This sod schoolhouse was built in Osborne County, Kansas. (KSHS)*

Dug-Out, Osborne County, Kans, 1879.

2.12. *Dugouts burrowed into the earth also served as schools on the frontier. (KSHS)*

burrowing into the side of a hill or ravine. These were so much a part of the earth that they were sometimes invisible from the opposite side of the hill. The doors of these buildings usually opened to the east, and whatever windows there were also had to be at the front of the building near the door. [Illus. 2.12]

In such schoolhouses, the first wave of homesteader children were educated with no thought of anything grander. There, amidst dirt walls and dirt floors, they learned how to read, write, and figure—and even a bit of Shakespeare. Some sod schoolhouses were still in use in the early twentieth century. But long before this, the pioneer period in the Midwest had passed, and almost everywhere the log and sod schoolhouses—symbols of the frontier—had been replaced by the little white frame buildings so fondly remembered by most midwesterners.

Chapter
3

The Little White Schoolhouse

3.1. *This cemetery just above the Crawfish River, southeast of Danville in Dodge County, Wisconsin, once lay within District No. 2, Elba Township.*

3.2. *The schoolhouse for District No. 2 in Elba Township, Dodge County, Wisconsin—later used for other purposes and now abandoned—stands diagonally across the road from the Catholic church and cemetery.*

In Dodge County, Wisconsin, a country road stretches south from the little village of Danville, turns to the southeast about half a mile from the village, then runs directly east toward the Crawfish River. A Catholic church and cemetery border this road on the north just before it reaches the river. [Illus. 3.1] To the south, diagonally opposite these landmarks, stands a one-room schoolhouse. In years gone by, this was the schoolhouse for District No. 2 of Elba Township. (For the location, see Illus. 1.3.) Like so many others of its kind, it was once converted to other uses but is now abandoned. Its small front door has been replaced by one that slides along a rail, and its windows have been boarded up. Unpainted and almost hidden in the foliage that surrounds it, it is scarcely noticeable to passersby. Even curious strangers find it hard to imagine that children once played here at recess and recited their lessons within its walls. In its time, however, it was a prim little one-room building bustling with active, eager children. That it has stood there in usable condition for nearly a century is a testament to its sturdy construction. [Illus. 3.2]

Most of the more than ninety thousand such

3.3. This architect's sketch of a country schoolhouse was drawn in 1867. Few midwestern farmers built their one-room schoolhouses from such sketches in the nine-teenth century. (State Archives of Michigan)

3.4. Motions made and adopted at specially called school meetings were the only blueprints for the farmers' one-room schools in the Mid-west. (Minutes, Dist. No. 2, Elba Twp., Dodge Co., Wis., School Records, SHSW)

schoolhouses that once blanketed the Midwest have disappeared. Some have been converted to other uses, but others, like the one in Elba District No. 2, stand unused and decaying along back roads, reminding those who deign to notice of a time when the education of children was the business of the whole community. At first glance, these little buildings—almost invariably painted white—seem so much alike that they appear to have been constructed from the same set of architectural plans. But this is not so. In fact, architects had very little to do with the design of midwestern country schoolhouses in the nineteenth century. To be sure, architects had been designing rural schoolhouses even before the Civil War and continued to do so into the twentieth century, when new schoolhouses were often built from their plans. But in the last half of the nineteenth century, few midwestern schools resembled an architect's fancy sketches. [Illus. 3.3]

Much to the disgust of county school superintendents and other school officials, who claimed that the one-room schoolhouses were "devised of total ignorance," midwestern farmers drew their own plans and debated them at their school meetings. Constructing schoolhouses was no more mysterious to them than building barns, houses, and granaries. No one had to explain to them about sills, studs, joists, shiplaps, or wainscoting. Such things were common knowledge on the farm. If they did need help they might consult their county superintendent, but they were just as likely to solve whatever problems arose by inspecting a neighboring schoolhouse.

In that small world, the building of a schoolhouse was a major community enterprise in which everyone had a voice. In this, as in so many rural undertakings, one can see the sometimes tangled processes of rural democracy un-

folding. Consider, for example, the construction of that little schoolhouse across from the Catholic church in Dodge County, Wisconsin. In the early summer of 1889, five of the district's leading farmers—men who at one time or another had served on the school board—petitioned the board to call a special meeting to discuss the building of a new schoolhouse. The meeting was held on July 15, and the farmers were presented with two choices: repair the old schoolhouse or build a new one.

Debate was undoubtedly lively, for farmers were not averse to speaking their minds, and subsequent events suggested that not everyone was in favor of a new schoolhouse. But the records are brief, and all we really know is that a majority voted to build a new schoolhouse and to approve the building's blueprint. They had no real blueprint, of course; all they had before them were suggested specifications, which were presented as motions, discussed, and voted on. This was precisely the way hundreds of one-room schoolhouses were built throughout the Midwest. [Illus. 3.4]

The district-to-district variations in building plans reflected in the minutes of school meetings illustrate how much midwestern farmers relied on their own initiative and how little on formal plans or blueprints in building their schoolhouses. The motions adopted by the farmers at the Sanford School, District No. 5, Woodstock Township, in Lenawee County, Michigan, in 1884, for example, concentrated on the building site and the school grounds and left many of the

3.5. Farmers in some school districts left the small details regarding the building of their schoolhouses to building committees. (Minutes, Dist. No. 5, Woodstock Twp., Lenawee Co., Mich., School Records in possession of Merton Dillon, Ohio State Univ.)

3.6. The Ise School in District No. 37, Osborne County, Kansas, illustrates the most common type of midwestern one-room schoolhouse: a plain rectangular building with three windows on each side and no embellishments of any kind.

details of the actual construction to a committee. [Illus. 3.5] Yet once the specifications had been agreed on, both this district and Elba, District No. 2, followed the usual pattern: both elected building committees to oversee the building of the schoolhouse.

Progress was not always unimpeded. Differences often surfaced about what kind of schoolhouse to build and how much to pay for it. Such was the price the farmers paid for democracy. In the great cities, these issues rarely raised an eyebrow, at least among the school's patrons. Schoolhouse construction there was someone else's problem. But in country districts, where the effects of building a new schoolhouse were immediately felt by everyone, no one's opinion could be ignored.

For reasons that are unclear, so much trouble surfaced in building Elba's District No. 2 schoolhouse that the first building committee and one school board member resigned. Shortly thereafter, a second special meeting was held to authorize the district to raise $550 to pay for the new schoolhouse. Nevertheless, when it was completed, District No. 2's schoolhouse was, as the farmers had specified, a "fraim house," twenty-two feet wide and thirty-two feet long. It had a stone foundation, three windows on each side, and a good pine floor. Smaller than many farm homes, it was as plain as the dirt road running past it. It had no shutters on its windows, no scrollwork to enhance its exterior trim, and no bell or belfry to break the outline of its roof.

Such plain schoolhouses existed everywhere throughout the Midwest after the Civil War, and many of them can still be seen. The Ise Schoolhouse in District No. 37, Osborne County, Kansas, is a good example. Built in 1884, when times were good, it was the district's third schoolhouse. It cost $600 to build and, like so many others built in the late nineteenth century, marked the progress of the tiny community from uncertainty to stability. Still, it had no distinguishing features, no embellishments, no ornamental trappings. Long since abandoned and in disrepair, it was still standing in the late 1980s beside a country road across from what had been Henry Ise's pasture, about a mile and a half northwest of the little town of Downs, Kansas. [Illus. 3.6]

The Ise Schoolhouse and, in fact, virtually all midwestern homes and small buildings built in the nineteenth century were balloon buildings. Few farmers ever knew it, but their one-room schoolhouses followed a design worked out by Augustine D. Taylor, a Chicago carpenter who invented balloon buildings in 1833. Hastily constructed in a matter of weeks around a framework of studs and sills, without the carefully wrought fittings that marked European buildings, they exemplified Americans' penchant for haste and proved so durable that even years of neglect have not completely destroyed them. [Illus. 3.7] Unrelieved by any adornment and nearly always rectangular, with three windows on each of the longer sides, these plain schoolhouses had a chimney at one end and a door, sometimes two, at the other. Many, like the Champion School in District No. 28, Logan County, Kansas, did not even have an anteroom

3.7. *Virtually all one-room schoolhouses were balloon houses, framed around studs anchored to sills. This is the Eminence School in Brown County, Indiana, after a fire. (Ind. Univ. Foundation)*

3.9. *Hamlin Garland remembered his schoolhouse as a "pine box" with two doors and three windows and "not a leaf to shade it in summer nor a branch to break the winds of savage winter." There were many just like it, such as the High Point School in District No. 12, Logan County, Kansas. (KSHS)*

where the children could hang their coats or an inner door to stave off wintry blasts. [Illus. 3.8]

Hamlin Garland likened his plain schoolhouse on the Iowa prairie to a "pine box," and the High Point School in District No. 12, Logan County, Kansas, was precisely the kind he described in *Son of the Middle Border.* "The schoolhouse which was to be the center of our social life," he wrote, "stood on the bare prairie about a mile to the southwest [of his home] and like thousands of similar buildings in the west, had not a leaf to shade it in summer nor a branch to break the winds of savage winter. . . . It was merely a pine box painted a glaring white on the outside and desolate and drab within. . . . It had two doors on the eastern end and three windows on each side. . . . It was a barren temple of arts even to residents of Dry Run." [Illus. 3.9]

The plain schoolhouses in which thousands of Garland's and later generations were baptized with the three Rs lacked nearly every educa-

3.8. *In schoolhouses that were too poor to have an anteroom or a vestibule, such as the Champion School in District No. 28, Logan County, Kansas, children's wraps had to be hung in the classroom. (KSHS)*

tional refinement, and they had their critics. Did they reflect the farmers' stinginess or their poverty? Did they represent the farmers' lack of interest in the education of their children or their concern? Were they painted white instead of red because white paint was cheaper? And were they painted merely to preserve them or to make them attractive? Charges echoed endlessly through educational circles that the plain school reflected the former rather than the latter alternatives posed. The poor, plain country schoolhouse, they said, mirrored the farmers' lack of pride in their community and their unconcern about where or whether their children went to school or even what they learned.

But did it? Has any other class of Americans confronted by such uncertainties of life—farm prices, panics, weather, disease, and accidents, to name a few—ever made as great an effort to educate their children as did the midwestern farmers? The plain little schoolhouses located at thousands of crossroads across midwestern valleys and prairies surely testified to their determination to see that their children could read and write.

Still, the critics had a point. In many midwestern localities—often in adjoining districts—two kinds of one-room schoolhouses could be found: one plain and the other, just down the road, improved. The four schoolhouses from the early 1900s shown in Illus. 3.10 illustrate the point. They were all in Cherry County, Nebraska, and

3.10. Did the farmers' degree of prosperity or interest in their children's education make the difference between those districts that maintained tidy, substantial schoolhouses and those that did not? Clockwise from the upper left, the schoolhouses in District Nos. 74, 60, 4, and 10, all in Cherry County, Nebraska, show a range of conditions. (NSHS)

3.11. A comparison of these schoolhouses in Chippewa County, Michigan, suggests that the farmers' interest in educating their children and community pride were more important than wealth in maintaining good schools. Pictured from top to bottom are the schoolhouses in District No. 7, Bruce Township; District No. 3, Sault St. Marie Township; and District No. 5, Bruce Township. (Sixty-first Annual Report of the Superintendent of Public Instruction of the State of Michigan, 1897 [Lansing, 1898], p. 61)

probably not too far from one another. District No. 60 (upper right) still clung to its sod schoolhouse and District No. 4 (bottom right) to its log school. District No. 74 (upper left) built a new frame schoolhouse to replace its soddie, shown crumbling behind it. The farmers in District No. 10 (lower left) showed the most care. They built a frame schoolhouse, added shutters to its windows, painted it, and dug a well. In fairness, however, the relative prosperity of these districts is unknown.

Perhaps the difference between caring and uncaring farmers is better illustrated by a comparison of three schoolhouses that Michigan's superintendent of public instruction found in Chippewa County on his 1897–98 tour. [Illus. 3.11] According to his report, the patrons of District No. 7 (top) were prosperous farmers, yet their schoolhouse was unpainted and neglected looking, both inside and out. When he saw it that year, it still had homemade desks, no dictionary, no flag, no curtains on the windows—nothing to make it attractive. The teacher was paid $35 a month, and the children roamed about the room at will. "Would that we could say something," he wrote, "to arouse the patrons of this district to a sense of their neglect!" He called the schoolhouse in District No. 5 (bottom) in Bruce Township "a pleasing contrast" to that in District No. 7. It had

a well-kept school yard, screened outbuildings, and a beautiful grove in back of the building. The teacher, who received the same salary as the teacher in District No. 7, had the attention and interest of the students. The best of the three schoolhouses, however, was the one in District No. 3 (middle), Sault St. Marie Township. It was, the superintendent wrote, substantial and well painted, and even its outbuildings were in fair condition, which was rare. Reputed to be one of the best-equipped schools in Chippewa County, it had neat curtains at its windows and a library of well-chosen books.

What made the difference in all these closely connected schoolhouses? In all likelihood, the appearance of each school was less a measure of the farmers' prosperity than their pride in their community, their aspirations for their children's advancement, and their interest in education. If they cared about these things, their schoolhouses were likely to have features that improved them and set them apart from plain schools.

To see one country school, then, was not to see them all. Even though they were all one-room affairs, the number of differences among them was surprising. Each one symbolized in its own way the midwestern farmers' desire—or lack thereof—to improve the quality of both their children's education and their own lives.

Chapter

4

Rural Aspirations

4.1. *Middle-class aspirations inspired many midwestern farmers to improve their one-room schoolhouses. An improved schoolhouse with shuttered windows built by Nebraska homesteaders in 1873 replaced a sod schoolhouse and affirmed the permanency of their community. District No. 40, Saunders County, Nebraska. (Courtesy of Mrs. Francis Beaman, Ceresco, Nebr.)*

The panic of 1873 loomed just above the horizon when the homesteaders in District No. 40, Saunders County, Nebraska, undertook a major project. There, not far from the little village of Ceresco, near the center of the farms they were wresting from the area's rolling hills, they built a new schoolhouse to replace the one they had fashioned from sod just four years before. Planned in the spring and built in the summer, the new schoolhouse was twenty-two feet wide and twenty-six feet long. It was really too small for the flock of children pictured in front of it, but it was not a typical one-room schoolhouse. [Illus. 4.1] It had interesting embellishments, including a transom over the door, a broad fascia one foot wide beneath the eaves, and a four-paned gable window. Shutters limned the windows, and the schoolhouse door, contrary to custom, was placed on the side rather than in the center of the building. If all the farmers' carefully drawn specifications were followed, it had slate blackboards, an anteroom inside the front door, and an inner door leading into the main room. Each of its eight-paned windows, equipped with proper springs, could be lowered from the top and raised from the bottom.

Standing in the middle of those newly claimed farms, the homesteaders' new schoolhouse was proof of their growing prosperity and progress. But it was more than that. It radiated an air of permanency that signaled the fixing of the district's wavering boundary lines, which had been pushed this way and that to accommodate new settlers. It meant, too, that the homesteaders, whose hold on the land had been tenuous, expected to stay where they had planted their roots. Indeed, some of their descendants are still there today.

This was no ordinary schoolhouse, and there was something about the character of the people who built it that was evident in the little building. With its shutters, gable window, and slate blackboards, it was the homesteaders' showpiece, reflecting the same dreams and white middle-class aspirations to "get ahead"—to say nothing of pretensions—that prompted small-town residents to build opera houses and libraries and large churches in the same period. But even if the school was built in part to impress neighboring districts and improve the district's social life, it was also a symbol of the farmers' determination to give their children a better education than they had had. This great aspiration was part of the midwesterners' legacy to us, and it has been realized in every generation of Americans until the present, when, according to *The Nation at Risk*, "for the first time . . . the educational skills of one generation will not surpass . . . will not even approach, those of their parents."

The cost of the new schoolhouse was a heavy burden. The farmers had contracted to build their schoolhouse for $546, but the added cost of building two privies and other necessities bonded their district for $700. Then came the financial panic of 1873. In the depression-ridden years ahead, their debt demanded the kinds of sacrifices that were never experienced by urbanites, who did not wrestle personally with the problems of building and paying for schoolhouses. Yet the district's farmers never wavered from their desire to give their children the best education they could. Three years after the completion of the building, they were still haunted by the panic and burdened by debt, but they wanted no cheap teacher. That year they voted—after some

4.2. *Typically, the anteroom of the Reed School in Chisago County, Minnesota, was visible from the outside only through the open door. (MHS)*

haggling, to be sure—to employ no teacher for the winter term who did not have at least a second-grade certificate.

In the years following the homesteaders' efforts to improve the District No. 40 schoolhouse, farmers in tens of thousands of other small districts across the Middle West were busily building new schoolhouses, repairing old ones, and adding a variety of improvements. Among such improvements were various kinds of porches and anterooms. Like the anteroom that can be seen through the open door in Illus. 4.2, the anteroom in District No. 40's schoolhouse was small. Nevertheless, it protected the classroom from wintry blasts and provided a boys' cloakroom on one side of the inner door and a girls' cloakroom on the other. For some districts, however, this outwardly invisible addition was not enough. To provide more room for their children's coats, hats, overshoes, and lunches, and to secure more privacy for the boys and girls, they added vestibules to their schoolhouses. And although this was not the purpose, these small additions relieved the architectural plainness of the schoolhouses.

Long remembered by country schoolchildren for the incidents that took place there at recess and noontime—the boys' scuffles and the passing of love notes—vestibules ranged from the simple

4.3. Its vestibule distinguished the improved String-town School in District No. 100, Greenwood County, Kansas, from common rectangular buildings. It provided good lighting and two rooms but reduced the usable wall space. (Walter M. Anderson Collection, Emporia, Kans.)

4.4. Less light and more usable space were features of the vestibule of the once nicely improved but now sadly neglected Parker Schoolhouse in Parker Township, Marshall County, Minnesota. (MHS)

to the ornate. The one attached to the Stringtown School in District No. 100, Greenwood County, Kansas, was typical of many. Two windows brightened the little room but took away some of the wall space available for coats and caps. Still, it gave the schoolhouse two rooms, in effect, and distinguished it from the ordinary rectangular buildings. [Illus. 4.3]

Unlike the one at the Stringtown School, the vestibule of the Parker Schoolhouse in Parker Township, Marshall County, Minnesota, had a transom over the door. It provided less light but more usable space. [Illus. 4.4] Built with care, this schoolhouse had broad fascia boards beneath the eaves of the roofs of both schoolroom and vestibule, a substantial porch, and a gutter and downspout along the eaves, which was unusual in one-room schoolhouses. No doubt it was once the pride of the community, and one can only speculate about whether poverty or carelessness, or perhaps both, was responsible for its unpainted and neglected appearance when it was photographed in 1904.

The growing desirability of separating boys' and girls' cloakrooms in improved schoolhouses was evident in the Prairie Valley Schoolhouse in District No. 7, Chariton County, Missouri. Built near the beginning of the new century, this schoolhouse featured a large porch, ornate pillars, and two doors leading into two vestibules,

thereby segregating the sexes to the extent possible in a one-room school. When the photograph was taken in about 1908, each vestibule had a washbasin, soap, and towels. [Illus. 4.5]

Along the Middle Border, however, few vestibules were more decorative than the one attached to the small schoolhouse in Union Township, Tippecanoe County, Indiana. With its shuttered vestibule windows facing out to the road, transom above the door, and ornamented gable window, it was unique among country schoolhouses. [Illus. 4.6] The ornate exterior of this

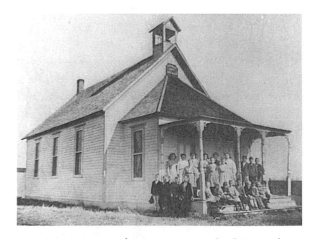

4.5. A growing emphasis on privacy for boys and girls was reflected in the two vestibules and two doors opening on the porch of this schoolhouse in District No. 7, Chariton County, Missouri. (Sixtieth Report of the Superintendent of Public Instruction, Missouri, 1908 [Jefferson City, 1909], opp. p. 31)

4.6. *The skill and imagination of a local craftsman are reflected in the vestibule of the schoolhouse in District No. 1, Union Township, Tippecanoe County, Indiana. (TCHA Archives)*

4.7. *Twenty-three years after building the Emery School, the farmers voted to add a bell and belfry. (Minutes, Dist. No. 3, Albion Twp., Dane Co., Wis., School Records, SHSW)*

schoolhouse was attributable to the skill and, no doubt, the whim of the local carpenter who built it. The intricate design at the high point of the vestibule, like so many of the flourishes added to improved schoolhouses, depended less on the farmers' plans than on rural carpenters' imaginations. Their names have been lost to history, but they left a rich legacy for those who cared about the appearance of their little schoolhouses.

Most farmers probably took no more notice of the artistry and skill of these anonymous rural craftsmen than did later generations, for few thought of country schoolhouses as works of art. Nevertheless, their creativity was visible on hundreds of midwestern one-room schoolhouses. Sometimes the mere scrollwork on the buildings reflected it. More often it was evident in the belfries that housed the schools' big bells. These big bells and belfries were the most obvious characteristics of improved schoolhouses in the late nineteenth and early twentieth centuries. In time, they became so common that contemporary sketches of country schools almost invariably include them. But they were not really as prevalent as might be supposed. Thousands of plain schoolhouses never had them, and many of those that did acquired them long after the schoolhouses had been built. Indeed, in the 1890s and early 1900s, farmers in district after district voted to install bells and belfries on their schoolhouses. It was twenty-three years after they had

built their schoolhouse that the farmers at the Emery School in District No. 3, Albion Township, Dane County, Wisconsin, voted to add a bell and belfry to their schoolhouse. [Illus. 4.7]

Midwestern country schoolhouses, like the farmers who built them, were nothing if not practical, which made the addition of these big bells something of a mystery. They were not especially practical, and they certainly were not necessary. Small hand bells and even rulers slapped against the schoolhouse had always been enough to bring the children in from play. Nor was there any law demanding that one-room schools have large bells. If they were not practical, necessary, or required, then why the big bells?

Farmers never really gave their reasons—or at least their reasons were not recorded in the minutes of their meetings. They might have argued that big bells could be used to hurry loitering children on their way to school in the morning, or to bring them back to the school yard when they wandered away at the noon hour. But this is doubtful. In the beginning, the idea of great school bells probably came from church bells. Perhaps big bells were first placed on schoolhouses that doubled as churches; in time, others acquired them as well. This seems to be a logical progression, since, at least until World War I, Americans considered schools to be almost sacred places, where people automatically spoke more quietly and watched their behavior.

4.8. *Buildings like the Antelope School in Logan County, Kansas, which served as both schoolhouse and church, may have been the first schoolhouses to have big bells and belfries. (KSHS)*

4.10. *Abandoned rural schoolhouses still stand next to active churches in the Midwest, such as the one in Pottawatomie County, Iowa.*

This is not as strange as it seems today. In the past, there was always a close connection between religion and education in the American experience. So common was this bond that the sponsors of the Ordinance of 1785, which set aside section sixteen for school purposes, had originally proposed that the section just north of it be used to support religion. Through the years, this connection has virtually disappeared—indeed, been made impossible. But it has been less than a century since religion and education were as closely linked in the American mind as free enterprise and democracy. Certainly that was true in the rural Midwest, where one-room schools often served as churches on Sundays. [Illus. 4.8] And in places where these twin agencies of civilization abided in separate buildings, they were frequently located side by side—virtual adjuncts to each other. [Illus. 4.9] Even today, they can be found standing together in their original locations. Usually the schoolhouse has been abandoned and neglected, but surprisingly, many of the churches are still active. [Illus. 4.10]

Of course, the farmers' decisions to purchase big bells for their schoolhouses, like other improvements they made, were surely prompted

4.9. *Schoolhouses and churches—twin agencies of civilization—frequently sat side by side in the Midwest, as did the ones in Clark County, Ohio. (OHS)*

in part by their aspirations to have schoolhouses that were comparable to or better than the schoolhouses in neighboring districts. It was probably no coincidence that the farmers in District No. 3, Albion Township, added a bell seven years after the neighboring district, Joint District No. 2 in Albion and Sumner townships, had done the same. Competition was the inspiration for much of the progress in these small midwestern communities, and no doubt wily bell salesmen took advantage of it, convincing farmers that they must have bells because neighboring districts had them. Whatever their motives, the farmers' addition of bells and belfries to their schoolhouses reflected their desire to improve their schoolhouses and communities rather than their practicality. As it turned out, the big bells were rarely used to ring the children in, but they were surely proud signs of progress and prosperity and the end of frontier conditions.

For a people with so little, the bells were not cheap. The price depended on the weight of the bell. In 1895, Montgomery Ward priced school bells from $7.50 to $25.00 or higher, if a real church bell was desired. When the cost of a bell hanging, which permitted the bell to swing, was added to the price of the bell, the total was enough to cause frugal farmers to hesitate months or even years before buying. [Illus. 4.11] Time was when farmers would never even have considered such luxuries, but times had changed. At the end of the century, it was evident everywhere across the region, from Ohio to Nebraska. Communities had stabilized, new homes and churches had been built, general stores stood at the crossroads, and expenditures for school improvements—even for such luxuries as bells—were within reach.

4.11. *School bell hangings were not included in the price of the bell and were costly in school districts where $1 was no small sum. (Whi [X3] 43028, SHSW)*

4.13. *The big bell atop the scaffold at the Burnside School in Marshall County, Kansas, reflects the people's aspirations and pretensions. (KSHS)*

Once the bells were purchased, some districts either could not afford to erect belfries in which to house them or for some other reason chose not to. Here and there, bells were simply fastened to poles erected just outside the schoolroom doors. [Illus. 4.12] Elsewhere, more elaborate structures were built for the bells. At the Burnside School in Marshall County, Kansas, the farmers built a sturdy scaffold for their bell near the schoolhouse porch. [Illus. 4.13] Few photographs better illustrate the midwestern farmers' aspirations—or pretensions, perhaps—than this picture of a big bell resting on a homemade derrick-like platform planted at the corner of a forlorn little schoolhouse on the Kansas plains. Surely such a school had no real need for a bell—only the farmers' need to show the world that they too could afford a bell for their children's school, even if they could not afford a belfry.

But if some schools had bells but no belfries, others had belfries but no bells. Early in the new century, belfries had become so much a part of the school architecture that some school districts obviously thought that they had to have one whether they had a bell or not. Many might have been too poor to afford both; others might have thought that a big bell was unnecessary; and still others might have hoped to add a bell later. In any case, the belfries on such schoolhouses, not the bells, became the symbol of the farmers' aspirations to improve their schools. [Illus. 4.14] Commonly, of course, rooftop belfries did house big bells. Ropes were attached to the bells and

4.12. *Some school districts had a bell but no belfry, such as this schoolhouse in District No. 113, Lyon County, Kansas. (Walter M. Anderson Collection, Emporia, Kans.)*

4.14. *Some one-room schoolhouses had a bell but no belfry; others, like this schoolhouse in District No. 5, Logan County, Kansas, had a belfry but no bell, suggesting that the belfry alone had become a symbol of the farmers' aspirations. (KSHS)*

4.15. *A simple, frugally constructed belfry housed the big bell on the roof of the country schoolhouse in District No. 75, Lyon County, Kansas. (Walter M. Anderson Collection, Emporia, Kans.)*

4.17. *The work of a skilled craftsman is visible in the belfry and throughout the exterior of the Fairview Knoll Schoolhouse in Shawnee County, Kansas. (KSHS)*

extended through the ceiling to the entry or classroom. Pulling of the bell rope when occasion demanded it was a privilege often extended to dutiful students.

To the casual observer, belfries were much alike, but there were myriad differences among them. The simplest ones were similar to the one on the Butcher Schoolhouse in District No. 75, Lyon County, Kansas. It was little more than four upright poles firmly anchored to a wood base straddling the top of the schoolhouse. These supported a small pointed cover for the bell. Unpre-

4.16. *A latticed enclosure added an artistic touch to the belfry on this Minnesota schoolhouse in District No. 95, Hennepin County. (Minn. State Dept. of Education)*

tentious yet neat, the Butcher School belfry was typical of many others seen on midwestern country schools in the late nineteenth and early twentieth centuries. [Illus. 4.15]

Other school belfries were as different from one another as the men who built them, mirroring their artistry and perhaps their philosophy about what they were building. To distinguish the belfries they built from the ordinary, some carpenters added only modest flourishes. The latticework atop the District No. 95 schoolhouse in Hennepin County, Minnesota, for example, was simple yet uncommon. [Illus. 4.16] Others took greater pains. Did the artisan who fashioned the belfry on the Fairview Knoll Schoolhouse in Shawnee County, Kansas, have a model for the delicately pointed triangles that formed the roof of the belfry and the large pillars that supported it, or were these the harvest of his own imagination? If so, did they represent anything more than a pretty design? We will never know, but here was an improved schoolhouse that illustrated both the creativity of rural craftsmen and the aspirations of farmers. It had shutters for all its windows, two front windows, intricate scrollwork beneath the eaves, and two doors, above which the design of the belfry roof was repeated. [Illus. 4.17]

For size, no belfries matched those on some Indiana schools. Unlike the belfries on most country schoolhouses, these were doubtless built

4.18. *Unlike the belfries on most midwestern one-room schoolhouses, the large walk-around belfries on some rural Indiana schools were designed by architects, such as the one in Roll, Indiana. (Blackford County–Beeson Collection, Ind. State Library, Ind. Div. Picture Collection)*

from an architect's sketch. They were large walk-around belfries constructed so that the schoolhouse resembled a church, reminding observers that the school was a temple of learning. [Illus. 4.18]

In time, some carpenters enclosed schoolhouse belfries with louvers. This was probably done more to protect the bell than for beauty, but by the early 1900s, the enclosed belfry had become commonplace. Like open belfries, these too were of different designs. Some, like the one erected on the schoolhouse in District No. 1, Logan County, Kansas, matched the design of the building and were obviously built when the schoolhouse was constructed. [Illus. 4.19] Most of the louvered belfries, however, were probably afterthoughts, built when the district decided to add a bell to the schoolhouse. The one on the Fairview School in District No. 82, Shawnee County, Kansas, was probably a later addition and is obviously quite different from the belfry in Illus. 4.19. Still, with its tapering roof leading to a spire, it was not at all uncommon. [Illus. 4.20]

The spire that so often ascended from the belfries of one-room schools were like those on

4.19. *The louvered belfry matching the design of this schoolhouse (District No. 1, Logan County, Kansas) was obviously no afterthought, but part of the original construction. (KSHS)*

country churches, but they had a different purpose. The church spire was obviously intended to complete the steeple reaching up to God, but on one-room schools they became flagpoles. About the time farmers were adding bells and belfries to their schoolhouses in the 1890s and early 1900s, flags became important in the rural Midwest. By this time the nation had rounded out a hundred years of its existence, and a wave of patriotism was sweeping the country. Children were just learning to recite the Pledge of Allegiance, composed by Francis Bellamy in 1892, and flags were flying over public buildings everywhere.

Nowhere was this patriotic fervor more visible and unabashed than in the rural heartland, where

4.20. *The tapered roof on this louvered belfry is capped by a spire, reminiscent of a church steeple. Fairview School, District No. 82, Shawnee County, Kansas. (KSHS)*

4.21. Nine years after building their school across from the Catholic church, the farmers in this district voted to have a flag. (Minutes, Dist. No. 2, Elba Twp., Dodge Co., Wis., School Records, SHSW)

4.22. Where stone was plentiful, farmers often built stone schoolhouses. Lower Fox Creek School, Chase County, Kansas.

4.23. Besides the typical white frame and occasional stone schoolhouses, some midwestern school districts had fine brick schools. Maple Grove School, District No. 8, Berrien Township, Berrien County, Michigan. (Sixty-first Annual Report of the Superintendent of Public Instruction of the State of Michigan, 1897 [Lansing, 1898], p. 52)

the very land under the farmers' feet had been a gift—or near gift—from a prodigal government. Across the region, in one school meeting after another, farmers voted to buy flags and erect flagpoles so that their children might pledge their allegiance. It was nine years after they built their little school across from the Catholic church in Dodge County, Wisconsin, that the farmers in Elba District No. 2 finally voted to erect a flagpole and appointed a committee to take care of it. [Illus. 4.21]

The belfry spire made an ideal flagpole. With a pulley at its top and two ropes—one with a flag attached—extending to the ground, it was easy to raise the flag to the lofty height above the belfry. It was kept there by tethering the rope to a stake in the ground. By the turn of the century, Old Glory waved over thousands of little schoolhouses from the hills and valleys of Ohio to the Kansas prairie.

Vestibules, bells, and belfries all helped improve midwestern one-room schoolhouses and set them apart from the plain and ordinary. Also different—and a vast improvement over Hamlin Garland's "little pine boxes"—were the stone and brick one-room schoolhouses located here and there throughout the Midwest. Even though such schoolhouses were more costly, midwestern farmers were not averse to building them, especially where brick and stone were easily accessible. In the limestone region of Kansas, for example, there were a number of stone schoolhouses, some still in use for meetings of one kind

or another. The sturdy Lower Fox Creek stone schoolhouse, overlooking Highway 177 in Chase County, Kansas, was built in 1882. Refurbished in 1972, it retains the sturdy aura of permanency the farmers gave it more than a century ago. [Illus. 4.22]

More numerous than stone schoolhouses were those made of brick. They were scattered throughout the Midwest, especially in Indiana and in older parts of the region. A few were built not long after the Civil War. Less than a decade

4.24. *This brick schoolhouse was built in 1897 and cost $2,000. It was the third schoolhouse in Fractional District No. 8, Claybank Township, Oceana County, Michigan.* (Sixty-first Annual Report of the Superintendent of Public Instruction of the State of Michigan, 1897 *[Lansing, 1898], p. 40)*

4.25. *The schoolhouses pictured here were followed by a brick building (not shown). They signify the evolution and prosperity of the rural community in District No. 5, Madison Township, Jay County, Indiana.* (Twenty-eighth Biennial Report of the State Superintendent of Public Instruction, Indiana, 1915–1916 *[Fort Wayne, 1917], p. 377)*

after that conflict, the farmers in District No. 8, Berrien Township, Berrien County, Michigan, built a fine brick schoolhouse at a cost far exceeding what it would have cost in the 1890s. Shaded by old, widely spaced maple trees, it was called the Maple Grove School and seated thirty-six students. It had two doors and a center window with an alcove behind it, opening into the main room. On either side of the alcove were small vestibules for the girls and boys. [Illus. 4.23]

In the last decade of the nineteenth century, when districts sometimes built new schoolhouses instead of repairing the old, brick became a more common building material. This evolution of schoolhouses and communities can be seen in Fractional District No. 8, Claybank Township, Oceana County, Michigan. This was one of the earliest districts organized in the county, and its first schoolhouse was a log cabin costing $75. A $400 frame building replaced this, and in 1897, the farmers built the brick schoolhouse shown in Illus. 4.24 for $2,000. The same evolution of a rural community from its pioneer origins to prosperous stability can be traced through the schoolhouses in District No. 5, Jay County, Indiana. In this district, the log schoolhouse yielded to the frame building standing beside it. At the

time the photograph was taken, the frame building was about to be replaced by a brick schoolhouse. [Illus. 4.25]

At the dawn of the new century, although thousands of one-room schoolhouses were still as plain as the day they were built, thousands more had been improved in one way or another. Very rarely, however, had there been any attempt to change the basic structure of the one-room building. True, an octagonal schoolhouse had been built in Plain Township in Kosciusko County, Indiana, in 1864. [Illus. 4.26] And in McLeod County, Minnesota, a later version of this style of architecture—replete with pillared porch and attractive bell and belfry—had been constructed. [Illus. 4.27] There were others too, but they apparently held no more attraction for the midwestern farmers than did the octagonal houses being built during the same period. Nor did they appeal to the immigrants—the Germans, Scandinavians, Bohemians, French Canadians, and others—who streamed into midwestern lands after the Civil War and participated in the building of schoolhouses.

One might have supposed that immigrants would tend to build schoolhouses that were similar to the buildings they had known in their homelands, but this rarely occurred. A country

4.26. *By 1915, this octagonal schoolhouse, built in 1864, was used only for church services. Eight-Square Schoolhouse, Plain Township, Kosciusko County, Indiana.* (Twenty-eighth Biennial Report of the State Superintendent of Public Instruction, Indiana, 1915–1916 *[Fort Wayne, 1917], p. 377)*

4.27. *This version of an octagonal schoolhouse was used well into the twentieth century. Octagon House, McLeod County, Minnesota. (MHS)*

4.28. *Most unusual for midwestern one-room schools was this French colonial design in Morrison County, Minnesota. (MHS)*

4.29. *The assimilation of immigrant children into the American mainstream through the one-room school experience was evidenced by the architecture of their schoolhouses. This Bohemian schoolhouse was indistinguishable from many another midwestern one-room school. East School, District No. 10, Ellsworth County, Kansas. (KSHS)*

schoolhouse in Morrison County, Minnesota, was modeled in part on the French colonial style, but it was still basically a one-room structure with three windows on each side and a chimney in the rear. [Illus. 4.28] Schoolhouses built in other immigrant districts were not much different from those built elsewhere. The Bohemian schoolhouse near Wilson, Kansas—with its bell, belfry, and two front windows—had no features that might distinguish it as an immigrant schoolhouse. [Illus. 4.29] Neither would a passerby in 1895 have seen anything Scandinavian about the Swedish schoolhouse in Subdistrict No. 1, Bates Township, Iron County, Michigan. [Illus. 4.30]

This sameness was a tribute to the one-room school's role in the process of assimilating immigrants into American society. Pushing into the American heartland, immigrants found strange laws requiring them to educate their children, create small school districts, and build their own

4.30. The forty-foot flagpole in the school yard of this Swedish school in Michigan—painted red, white, and blue—denotes the residents' acceptance of American ways. Subdistrict No. 1, Bates Township, Iron County, Michigan. (Sixty-first Annual Report of the State Superintendent of Public Instruction of the State of Michigan, 1897 [Lansing, 1898], p. 74)

schoolhouses. And just as the children who attended those schools were being brought into the American mainstream by the lessons they learned there, the structures of their schoolhouses demonstrated the same kind of assimilation.

Aside from the schoolhouse itself, perhaps no better measure of the success of this process existed than the forty-foot-tall red, white, and blue flagpole standing just outside the door of the Swedish schoolhouse pictured in Illus. 4.30. The schoolhouse, with its big bell, belfry, and porch, was an improved building that, according to the Michigan state superintendent, betokened the Swedish immigrants' "interest in the welfare of their children." And this was true of nearly all those who improved their schoolhouses, even when their motives for doing so were mixed with their middle-class aspirations.

Another, perhaps more important, indication of the farmers' interest in their children's education was the refinements they made in the classrooms and around the school yards as the nineteenth century wore on.

Chapter
5

In and Out of the Country Schoolhouse

5.1. *The Collins School in Reed's Lake, Michigan, had a typical midwestern country school classroom. No ghetto schoolroom in modern times provides a more unlikely learning environment. (State Archives of Michigan)*

Having spent some eight years of their young lives within its confines, few midwestern country children ever forgot the appearance of their schoolroom. Long after they had left it to make their way in the world, they could close their eyes and see the big stove in the center of the room, the stovepipe latched to the ceiling, the big double desks in which they sat, and the creaky pine floor beneath their feet. They could imagine the blackboard behind the teacher's desk, see the wainscoting circling the room some three feet above the floor, feel the sun pouring through the windows, and smell the musty odor rising from the books, the chalk, and the oiled floors. [Illus. 5.1]

No ghetto schoolroom in modern times ever provided a more unlikely learning environment than this one-room country classroom. It was so small that a spitball could be shot from one end to the other, and so ill heated and ill lighted by modern standards that it would be considered unhealthy, unsafe, and unbearable today. Even at its best, it was no match for the worst of to-day's urban schoolrooms. Unfortunately, in 1900, many were not at their best, even though they had been improved through the years.

5.2. The trampling of children's feet through the years warped the floors of many one-room schoolrooms by 1900. (Minn. State Dept. of Education)

The new century had not yet spent its second year when Nebraska's superintendent of public instruction reported on his recent tour of the state's one-room schoolrooms. His appraisal was not encouraging. In school after school he had seen grimy walls, smoky lampshades, a scarcity of slate blackboards, rattletrap desks, and warped floorboards. [Illus. 5.2] In some schools, teachers who were desperate to decorate the walls and make them attractive had used advertisements of McCormick's harvester, Hood's sarsaparilla, and Pear's soap for the purpose.

Not long after the superintendent's trip, a journalist for *World's Work* found a school in Winnebago County, Illinois, not unlike those the superintendent had described. Located only a few miles from Rockford, it was called the worst school in the county. Large holes marred its outer walls, and only a thin partition separated the children from the snow and rain outside. Inside, the homemade desks were worn and battered; one had lost its seat, and another sagged from its supports. Overhead, soot leaked from the stovepipe. [Illus. 5.3] Grimy walls, warped floors, battered seats, and leaky stovepipes—defects that could have been easily and inexpensively repaired—offered substantial proof that midwestern farmers were not really concerned about the education of their children. The evidence seemed irrefutable.

But what was true of some farmers in some districts was not true of all farmers in all districts. The Winnebago County example was,

after all, the worst school in the county. And those that the Nebraska state superintendent described had been chosen for their flaws, to show the need for change. To be sure, there were more than enough bad schools in every state to cause concern, but most midwestern country schoolrooms near the turn of the century were better than they had been twenty years earlier. Most reflected the farmers' desire to do what they could with their limited resources to make their children's schoolrooms as attractive and comfortable as their own homes.

It was simply not true that the region's farmers paid no attention to the cleanliness of schoolrooms. In thousands of districts across the region, no annual school meeting adjourned until motions had been passed to clean the schoolhouse, patch the walls, repair the stovepipe, and

5.3. This was the worst schoolhouse in Winnebago County, Illinois. Neglect of one-room schools seemed to prove the critics' charge that midwestern farmers lacked interest in improving their children's education. (World's Work, vol. 8 [June 1904], p. 4889)

5.4. *The efforts of farmers in the Midwest to clean, repair, and improve their schoolrooms were verified in the reports of school district treasurers. (Dist. No. 5, Woodstock Twp., Lenawee Co., Mich., School Records in possession of Merton Dillon, Ohio State Univ.)*

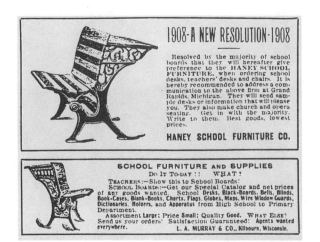

5.5. *For many years, patented school desks that replaced the homemade variety were constructed with a desktop attached to the back of the seat. (American School Board Journal, vol. 36 [Feb. 1908], n.p.)*

make whatever other repairs were needed before the beginning of the school term. Proof that such motions were not neglected showed up year after year in the ledgers of the district treasurers, who paid the bills and helped make sure that the work was done. [Illus. 5.4]

Just as there were farmers throughout the 1880s and 1890s who improved their schoolhouses with bells and belfries and vestibules, there were those who made important additions to their schoolrooms that changed them from pioneer schools to permanent elementary schools. For example, no more than a handful of midwestern one-room schoolrooms still had homemade desks by 1900. Trying to keep abreast of the changing world and driven by the admonitions of county superintendents, their pride, and competition with other schools, midwestern farmers were already installing patented desks to replace homemade ones in the 1870s. At first the new desks tended to be double-seated, perhaps to permit two children to use the same book or to conform to the then-popular theory that it helped the learning process to have children study together. These were gradually replaced with single desks that consisted of a seat with a desktop attached to its back. [Illus. 5.5] This necessitated placing the desks in straight rows, one behind the other, so that one seat was behind each desktop. The farmers then nailed them to the floor or to extra boards. When the front of the row near the teacher's desk was reached, seats were left without desktops. These were sometimes used by the children when they came forward to recite. [Illus. 5.6]

Besides new desks, the typical midwestern country school of the early 1900s did have slate blackboards, despite the Nebraska superintendent's report to the contrary. The little Sanford School in District No. 5, Woodstock Township, Lenawee County, Michigan, had them as early as 1889 and paid $1.50 to have them hung (see Illus. 5.4). Nor were all the lamp chimneys dim with smoke. Near the end of the 1890s, many rural classrooms that were once devoid of artificial lights were equipped with the latest in

5.6. *Seats were placed one behind the other and nailed to the floor. At the front of each row, a seat was left without a desktop. (SHSI, Iowa City, E. M. Clark Collection)*

kerosene lamps—specially devised for school-rooms or public buildings. They often had reflectors behind them that illuminated school programs and socials with a brightness that patrons were unaccustomed to in their homes. Some of the lamps were held by brackets extending from the wall; others hung from the ceiling and could be pulled down for cleaning. In either case, their glass chimneys were usually rubbed clean, at least before an evening function at the schoolhouse. Such lamps, like the school belfry, were another sign of community progress.

Smaller, less costly improvements that had been put off were eventually made to enhance the attractiveness of country schoolrooms. It took time for some districts to purchase such simple additions as window shades, but by 1900 they were standard equipment in nearly every schoolroom. Curtains were an even later addition, but they too became commonplace in the new century as district women banded together to sew and hang them in their children's classrooms. [Illus. 5.7]

At about the same time, school boards were persuaded to invest in suitable wall pictures to replace those colorful illustrations of McCormick's harvester and Pear's soap. Many of these were bought from the Perry Pictures Company, which offered as many as 1,200 subjects. By the early 1900s, this company's reproductions of

5.8. *To decorate the walls of their classrooms, school boards bought pictures from the Perry Pictures Company, which offered 1,200 items for sale.* (American School Board Journal, *vol. 36 [Feb. 1908], p. xix*)

such paintings as *The Sower* and *The Gleaner*, as well as portraits of American heroes and biblical characters, could be seen on thousands of country school walls. [Illus. 5.8]

Changing times naturally brought changing views about what was needed in the one-room classroom, and as the years passed, midwestern school districts began to spend more and more money for articles that had long been commonplace in urban schoolrooms. Clocks, dictionaries, organs, and an array of "school apparatus" found their way into midwestern country classrooms. The school-supplies industry was just one of the flourishing new businesses that helped build the nation's great industrial empire, and it targeted both rural and urban schools with its advertisements and salesmen. School apparatus could be almost anything—from desks and slate blackboards to water pails and erasers—but mostly it meant globes and maps and various kinds of learning charts.

The midwestern one-room schools were an inviting market. Unlike urban schools, where professional educators were in charge of purchasing school supplies, the farmers' purchasing agents were the school board members. Inexperienced in such matters, many of them were no match for the school-supplies salesmen who swarmed on them in the 1890s like flies around a screen door on a cool summer day. Driving through the countryside in their buggies, the salesmen sought out school board members and, like modern computer salesmen, convinced them that charts and maps would make learning easy and enhance the children's education immeasurably. This was not difficult. If the board members did not know one chart from another, as their critics alleged, they were likely—as the salesmen

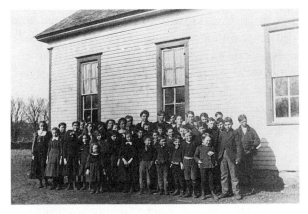

5.7. *Shades for the windows were standard equipment for midwestern schools by 1900. More concerned districts added curtains made by the district's women. Shell Rock School, Lyon County, Kansas.* (Walter M. Anderson Collection, Emporia, Kans.)

5.9. *The exterior of the schoolhouse in Subdistrict No. 4, Briley Township, Montmorency County, Michigan, does not appear to be extraordinary.* (Sixty-first Annual Report of the Superintendent of Public Instruction of the State of Michigan, 1897 [Lansing, 1898], p. 37)

5.11. *At the turn of the century, reading was encouraged in the Midwest's country schools by the acquisition of libraries. Commonly, all books in the library could be contained in one bookcase set against a wall, as in this schoolroom in Springfield Township, Clark County, Ohio. (OHS)*

5.10. *The interior of the schoolhouse in Subdistrict No. 4, Briley Township, Montmorency County, Michigan, displays the latest in school fixtures and apparatus—lamps, a physiological chart, a pictorial history chart, a clock, and an organ. (*Sixty-first Annual Report of the Superintendent of Public Instruction of the State of Michigan, 1897 [Lansing, 1898], p. 37)

knew they would be—to purchase anything to help their children's education.

Many of the changes enumerated above were obvious in the schoolroom in Subdistrict No. 4, Briley Township, Montmorency County, Michigan. Set in a wooded area in the northern part of the state, this little schoolhouse appeared to be quite ordinary from the outside. Just inside the front door it had an entryway running the width of the building but no shelves for books and no hooks for the children's wraps. [Illus. 5.9] The classroom had poor ventilation, and when the state superintendent visited in the winter of 1897, he found the room "tight as a drum," creating what he called "soporific conditions." Nevertheless, he reported that the room could seat about forty students and gave it high marks for its appearance and for the school apparatus he saw there. It was neat and cozy, well lighted, and equipped with a physiological chart for the study of hygiene and a pictorial chart for teaching history. It was also equipped with a clock, an organ, and the latest in kerosene lamps. [Illus. 5.10]

These acquisitions mirrored not only the burgeoning school-supplies business but also the midwestern countryside's advancing culture. Another indication of the region's growing sophistication were the libraries that had found a place in country schoolrooms by the end of the 1890s. Midwestern country school libraries had no separate rooms, of course, at least not before 1900. A bookcase along the wall held all the school's books, scarcely more than fifty or sixty. Among the titles were *Ben Hur*, *Pilgrim's Pro-*

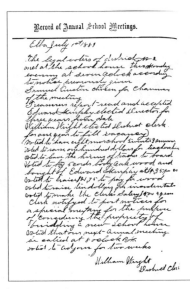

5.13. *Wood for the school's winter fuel was carefully stacked in the school yard or in a woodshed, if available. (State Archives of Michigan)*

5.12. *Each year at the annual school meeting, farmers contracted with one of their number to secure wood for the schoolroom stove. (Minutes, Dist. No. 2, Elba Twp., Dodge Co., Wis., School Records, SHSW)*

gress, and similar works. Many had a religious orientation, and farm children who spent hours reading books from their school libraries were as thoroughly indoctrinated in the period's moral earnestness as are today's children in the secular world. [Illus. 5.11]

Textbooks, however, were another matter. Midwestern states generally let each school district decide whether or not to furnish free textbooks to the children, and a vote was taken on the matter at every annual meeting. Although most districts had adopted a standard set of texts by the 1890s, they rarely voted to provide the books free of charge, except to the children of indigent parents. Rural midwesterners found it foreign to the doctrine of self-help to shift parental responsibilities to the community.

There were some things that the farmers could not easily change in their country schoolrooms. In the more than three decades since the Civil War, no substitute had been found for the big stove and its elongated stovepipe making its way across the ceiling. Standing imposingly in the front, rear, or center of the schoolroom, it remained the best remembered and most inclegant fixture. And it was not inexpensive to fuel. Where wood was available, it continued to be

sacrificed to the great stove into the twentieth century. Its acquisition was the responsibility of the man who won the wood contract at the annual meeting. [Illus. 5.12] He generally found, hauled, cut, and stacked the wood neatly in the school yard for the coming winter. [Illus. 5.13]

In the prairie states to the west, and increasingly in the older states as well, coal and corncobs warmed the farm children as they entered school on frosty mornings. This fuel was stored in bins or coal houses located near the schoolhouse and was retrieved by the older boys, whose chore it was to keep the coal bucket full. [Illus. 5.14] Apparently there was no contractual arrangement for the provision of fuel in the prairie states. Any one of several farmers might

5.14. *On winter days in the prairie states, where coal and corncobs fueled the school stove, older boys beat a path to the coal bin to keep the school's coal bucket filled. District No. 42, Logan County, Kansas. (KSHS)*

haul coal or corncobs to the schoolhouse. At least this was so in District No. 40, Saunders County, Nebraska, where three different men hauled 9,240 pounds of coal and three loads of corncobs to warm the schoolhouse in the harsh winter of 1884. [Illus. 5.15]

Whether they burned coal or wood or corncobs, however, the stoves generated so much heat and the schools were so tightly buttoned on frigid winter days that a lighted candle could scarcely burn. Aside from opening the door every now and then to bring in fresh air or placing a small stick beneath a window to keep it slightly open, the solution to the heating problem in most country schools still remained to be solved in the new century.

Likewise, the supply of water remained a problem resistant to change in many midwestern school districts. In nearly every midwestern country schoolroom in 1900, the water pail was still the prominent feature it had been thirty years earlier. Filled from the well of a neighboring farm, usually by the same boys who hauled in the coal, it was the only source of water in schools without wells of their own. Suspended over the bucket was the communal dipper from which the children drank their fill, innocent of the lurking danger in that practice.

5.16. By the early 1900s, iron pumps—like the one at the Fowler Schoolhouse in Lyon County, Kansas— were so common that they became as familiar as bells and belfries. Many districts, however, never had wells for their schools. (Walter M. Anderson Collection, Emporia, Kans.)

More was done to alleviate this problem, however, than had been done to change the heating system. As the old century moved on, one district after another developed its own water supply by drilling a well on school grounds. For these small districts, it was an expensive undertaking, and only the most prosperous or the most caring managed to do it. Hard-pressed after the building of their school in 1873, the farmers in District No. 40, Saunders County, Nebraska, waited eleven years before they bored a well in the school yard, at a cost of $16 (Illus. 5.15 lists this expense). As it turned out, eleven years was a comparatively short time to wait. A large number of country schools in the Midwest still had no well after seventy years! Yet so many districts had wells by the first decade of the new century that the old iron pump with its long handle became as familiar a fixture of the country school yard as the bell and belfry. [Illus. 5.16]

Wells ended the schools' complete dependence on the water pail, since the children could go to the well for a drink. But even where no school yard wells existed and the water pail remained, drinking patterns were not the same. More and more children were eschewing the common dipper and drinking from their own cups. But cup after cup dipped into the bucket was as unsani-

5.15. In the winter of 1884, three men from one district in Nebraska hauled 9,240 pounds of coal and three loads of corncobs to warm their schoolroom. (Treasurer's Report, Dist. No. 40, Saunders Co., Nebr., School Records, NSHS)

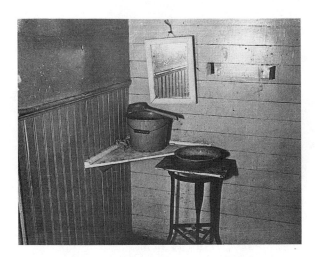

5.17. Washbasins and mirrors took their place beside the water pail and dipper as the culture of the countryside advanced. (Minn. State Dept. of Education)

tary as the common use of the dipper, and at least one Wisconsin district thought it necessary to adopt a motion ordering all children to use the dipper to fill their cups rather than dip them into the bucket.

The scene at the water pail had changed too. For years, country children had been taught that cleanliness was next to godliness. By 1900, the opportunity to practice what was preached was made possible by the addition of a washbasin, soap, mirror, and even a comb placed near the water pail. "We have everything very convenient," an eleven-year-old Kansas girl wrote in 1893. "We have mirrors, combs, towels, and a washbasin." [Illus. 5.17]

Farmers across the Middle West who had caught the spirit of change were also changing the appearance of their school yards. Often they began by attacking the privy problem that had so exasperated educators in the late nineteenth century. By 1900, two small outbuildings standing at the back corners of the school yard were standard, but they had not always been there. Some midwestern country schools, even in the 1880s, had no privies other than the trees to which the children fled in time of need. Other schools had only one privy, used first by the girls at recess time and then by the boys. Where two existed, they were sometimes built under one roof, which led one state superintendent to write that they furnished "exactly the right conditions to evoke

the obscene scrawls that so often deface the walls of similar places." [Illus. 5.18] Even where the two toilets were separated from each other, the boys' especially was likely to be filthy and in disrepair. Waste in the vaults frequently piled up almost to overflowing, and the seats were badly soiled. [Illus. 5.19] Besides that, some privies had been so vandalized that they could be used only if someone stood watch to ward off inquisitive mischief makers. The privy in Illus. 5.20, used by girls, boys, and the teacher, was not all that unusual.

Why so many farm families were not more sensitive to this problem remains a mystery. It was certainly not because they lacked modesty. In fact, rural women were so modest about bodily functions that a woman might refuse to go to the outdoor privy if a man other than her husband was in the yard. The explanation may be that the outhouses on their farms were little better than those on the school grounds. Whatever the reason, these "places of retirement," as they were euphemistically called, continued to be neglected through the years, in spite of many an educator's pointed philippic against this unhygienic and immodest condition.

5.18. Some midwestern country schools had no privies for years. Others had only one, and some had two under one roof, to the consternation of school officials. (OHS)

5.19. With soiled seats and overflowing vaults, the boys' privy was likely to be especially unsanitary. (Minn. State Dept. of Education)

5.20. This privy—used by all the students plus the teacher—was so vandalized and neglected that it could be used only if someone stood guard. (U.S. Bureau of Education, Bulletin no. 12 [Washington, D.C.: GPO, 1914], pl. 42)

5.21. In the best school districts, farmers built two privies and screened them with boards or bushes—symbols of victory for Victorian morals along the Middle Border. (SHSI, Des Moines)

But encouraged by the spirit of progress, the pervasiveness of Victorian morality, and the nagging of county superintendents, farmers finally confronted the problem. By 1900, most had built a privy where none had existed, or two where only one had been. Many were repaired, and some farmers even went so far as to shield their privies by solid wood barriers or foliage, which was, in a way, a symbol of victory for Victorian morality. [Illus. 5.21]

This improvement was frequently accompanied by a school yard beautification program. For years, the betterment of country school yards had not been a high priority with midwestern farmers. It was enough just to have a schoolhouse and the funds to maintain it. Children could play anywhere, and beauty—aside from that which nature provided free of charge—was an unaffordable luxury. Consequently, many school yards were small, rough pieces of land,

unfit for farming and donated by a farmer who wanted the schoolhouse to be located near his farm. Many of those that were level and reasonably large had no trees or bushes of any kind.

One impetus for the beautification program was a wonderful innovation called Arbor Day, a day set aside for the planting of trees. Suggested by the one-time governor of Nebraska in 1872, the idea spread rapidly across the Midwest just as new schools were being built and old ones repaired. Nowhere was it observed with more devotion than in the one-room schools of the Middle West. Arbor Day was a special day in country schools—an ecology day before we had such things—and parents and school board

5.22. This schoolhouse originally had no bell, no belfry, and no trees to shade its grounds. Subdistrict No. 7, Oneida Township, Delaware County, Iowa. (SHSI, Iowa City, Huftalen Collection)

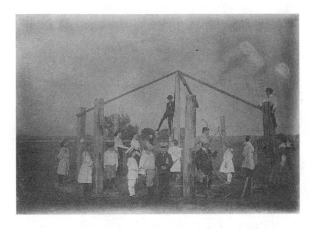

5.23. *Under the teacher's direction, the children built an arbor on the barren school grounds. Subdistrict No. 7, Oneida Township, Delaware County, Iowa. (SHSI, Iowa City, Huftalen Collection)*

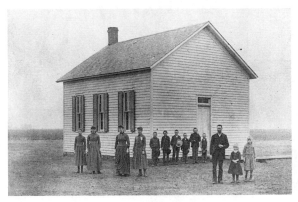

5.25. *Until the early 1900s, hundreds of unfenced school yards lay open to the prairie, forests, and farmers' fields that bordered them, as at this schoolhouse in Sedgwick County, Kansas. (KSHS)*

members alike were invited to the school to hear their children recite from George Pope Morris's poem:

> Woodmen spare that tree
> Touch not a single bough.
> In youth it sheltered me,
> And I'll protect it now.

Or sometimes, standing outdoors with the wind whipping through Old Glory, they asked, "What

5.24. *In time, a bell and belfry were added to the schoolhouse, arborvitae trees were planted on the school grounds, and the school was named the Arbor Vitae Summit School. Subdistrict No. 7, Oneida Township, Delaware County, Iowa. (SHSI, Iowa City, Huftalen Collection)*

do we plant when we plant a tree?" or declaimed the speeches of American notables. Whatever the program, in the end they planted a tree their parents had provided to help erase the barrenness of the school yard and provide shade for noontime lunches and play.

The evolution of school yard improvements was recorded in the early 1900s in photographs taken by a remarkable teacher in Subdistrict No. 7, Oneida Township, Delaware County, Iowa. When she first arrived there, the little school on the hill had no bell and the grounds had no trees. [Illus. 5.22] Not long thereafter, the children built an arbor under her direction. [Illus. 5.23] Eventually a bell and belfry—those twin symbols of rural aspiration—graced the schoolhouse roof, arborvitae trees were planted in the school yard, and the school boasted a big sign carrying the new name of the school: "ARBOR VITAE SUMMIT." [Illus. 5.24]

Barely visible in these photographs is the fence that surrounded the school yard. For years, country school yards were unfenced and open to the prairie, the forest, animal traffic, and the farmers' fields that bordered them. [Illus. 5.25] To have a beautiful school yard, however, a fence was almost a necessity. School improvement came to include the building of fences, ranging from attractive wooden structures to simple barbed wire. An unusual white picket fence set off the shaded school yard of the Townshend School, located on the old National Road in

5.26. *To help beautify their school yards, farmers built various kinds of fences around the grounds. A picket fence surrounded the yard of the Townshend School in Muskingum County, Ohio, on the old National Road. A milestone in the lower right corner of the photograph gives the distance from Columbus to Cumberland. (Bureau of Public Roads, NA)*

5.28. *Midwestern country school yards and fences, like improved and plain schools, presented a contrast between caring and uncaring school districts. The sagging fence and barren school yard around this schoolhouse suggest the failure to observe Arbor Day. Lauramie Township, Tippecanoe County, Indiana. (TCHA Archives)*

5.27. *The beautiful fence and school yard at this crossroads school in Indiana suggest the value of Arbor Day in the Midwest. District No. 5, Wea Township, Tippecanoe County, Indiana. (TCHA Archives)*

Muskingum County, Ohio. [Illus. 5.26] Another kind of wooden fence was that surrounding the Kenny School in District No. 5, Wea Township, Tippecanoe County, Indiana. It enhanced the beauty of this crossroads school, whose trim grounds and abundant trees suggested the success of more than one Arbor Day program. [Illus. 5.27] Unfortunately, few were kept as well as this, and some were hardly cared for at all.

The school yards and school fences of midwestern country schools, like improved and plain schools, presented the contrast between caring and uncaring districts. The sagging barbed wire fence and the bare school yard enclosing the improved schoolhouse in District No. 16, Lauramie Township, also in Tippecanoe County, contrasted sharply with that in District No. 5 in Wea Township. Here Arbor Day had obviously either gone unobserved or failed in its purpose. [Illus. 5.28]

Not everywhere across the Middle Border, of course, had all these changes—both inside and outside—taken place. In 1900, hundreds of midwestern schoolhouses still had no bells, no belfries, no window shutters, and no embellishments of any kind; their school yards had no trees, no pumps, no fences, and only shabby privies. Yet few had escaped some improvement: a new coat of paint perhaps; the addition of school apparatus, including dictionaries and globes; new desks; and nice pictures on the walls. No longer could they be considered pioneer schools. They were established schools in settled communities—the backbone of the midwestern educational system, and the fountain from which flowed many of the students who would fill the area's normal schools and universities. They were also the schools that many remembered so fondly as they looked back on their school days.

Chapter
6

School Days

6.1. "To see her self-reliance and independence," wrote an observer, "made one feel that any sympathy for her on account of her long ride, was entirely misplaced." (Twenty-Third Biennial Report of the State Superintendent of Public Instruction, Nebraska, 1913–1915 [Lincoln, 1914], p. 118)

6.2. If the way was long, some children, such as these students from Shawnee County, Kansas, rode to school in a buggy. (KSHS)

One day in 1913, an observer at the school house in District No. 17, Dawes County, Nebraska, watched as six-year-old Mildred Harris, no taller than the stirrup on her horse's saddle, mounted the animal by some uncanny maneuver and began the three-mile trip home. Evening and morning she made this trip throughout the school year, stopping on her way to open and close a gate. [Illus. 6.1]

Making their way to school was one of the great pleasures—and one of the great trials—long remembered by those who attended country schools in the Midwest. For many of them, it was an education in itself; for others, it was a test of their endurance and their desire to go to school. If the school was far away, they rode their ponies to school as Mildred did. Others harnessed their horses, hitched them to buggies or carts, and drove the long distance to school. [Illus. 6.2] But for most midwestern children, the schoolhouse was not quite so far away. Ideally it was located near the center of the district, which meant that most children would have to go no farther than a mile or two. The ideal, however, was not always obtainable, because the school site was often given to the district by a farmer whose farm

6.3. *From the late 1880s into the next century, the Ise children walked to school across this field. Still standing in the 1980s, the schoolhouse sits in the foreground; the Ise home is across the field.*

was not centrally located. And even when it was, it was bound to be closer to some children than to others.

For the Ise children, whose father, Henry, had given the land for the District No. 37 school in Osborne County, Kansas, the trip to school was a pleasant walk of no more than a quarter of a mile across the pasture from their home. [Illus. 6.3] But it was not without its occasional perils. One day, the children were caught in the kind of blinding blizzard of snow and dust that can

6.4. *"That road to school was wonderful; rich in color in autumn and tuneful with frogs in the spring." The writer might have been describing a road like this one near the Deckard School in Brown County, Indiana. (Ind. Univ. Foundation)*

sweep across the prairie at a moment's notice. So fierce was the storm that they could hear only the wind and see only swirls of snow. Lost and circling about in the great storm, they were rescued by their father, who stumbled upon them and led them to the fence line, which they followed to the farmhouse.

Through the 1880s and well into the 1900s, Henry and Rosie Ise watched their eleven children make their way back and forth across the pasture to the schoolhouse, until finally the last one completed school there. "When Dutch finished his last year in the little schoolhouse," John Ise wrote in *Sod and Stubble*, his semifictional account of his family's life on the plains, "and came home with his books and slate tied in a bundle of twine, she [Rosie] sat down and had a good cry to think that she would never again look out beyond the corral and across the pasture, to see the children come trudging home."

For most country children, however, the path to school lay along country roads rather than across a pasture. Each school day they could be seen walking along in twos and threes, lunch pails and perhaps their slates and a book or two in hand, inching toward the schoolhouse, which seemed—to the very young at least—to be at the end of the world. On warm summer and autumn days, they often lingered along the road, which was alive with intriguing curiosities. Sometimes they stopped to catch a butterfly or pick a flower, watch a snake slither through the grass, or simply to play. "That road to school," wrote the eminent scientist Marshall Barber in *The Schoolhouse at Prairie View*, "was wonderful; rich in color in autumn and tuneful with frogs in spring—I remember every yard of it as it was when I was a child." [Illus. 6.4]

But in the spring, when the snows melted and the rains fell and the dirt roads became quagmires, simply wading through the mud was enough to consume whatever spare time and energy the children had. And this was doubly true in winter. [Illus. 6.5] Country schools rarely closed for winter storms unless there was a blizzard yowling through the countryside. Snow itself, piled high across the roads, was not enough to shut down the school. Midwestern rural children often set off for school through

6.5. *Spring thaws and rains made the road to the schoolhouse in Lyon County, Kansas, a muddy slough from fence to fence. (Walter M. Anderson Collection, Emporia, Kans.)*

6.6. *In winter, the children often set off for school through snowdrifts piled high beside the road. (Amer-*ican Monthly Review of Reviews *26 [Dec. 1902], p. 704)*

6.7. *Shy and fearful, Herbert Quick cried uncontrollably when he entered this school, which is now located in Grundy Center, Iowa.*

snowdrifts that were waist high and sometimes over the heads of the smaller folks. In *Son of the Middle Border*, Hamlin Garland recalled how he and his companions braved the snowdrifts in Iowa in the 1870s: "Facing the cutting wind, wallowing through drifts, battling like some intrepid animal, we often arrived at the door moaning with pain yet unsubdued, our ears frosted, our toes numb in our boots, to meet others in similar case around the roaring stove." [Illus. 6.6]

Such passion for getting to school is hard to believe today, when so little physical effort is needed and education is taken for granted. But rural children had reasons for going to school that would be largely incomprehensible to their contemporary urban counterparts. For one thing, many of them actually liked school. They liked the excitement of spell-downs and cipher-downs and declamations. They enjoyed those occasions when they all piled into a sleigh or buggy to visit the school in the next district. In the books they read they discovered far-away places and dramatic events that brought the world into their circumscribed lives. School fed their imaginations, and Hamlin Garland spoke for many of them when he wrote, "we were fond of school and never missed a day if we could help it."

There were other reasons, too, for wanting to go to school. For some—perhaps a large number—school was preferable to the hard work that awaited them if they stayed home. Beyond that,

the loneliness of farm life made going to school attractive. Unlike urban children who had friends next door, playgrounds down the street, and the hubbub of the busy city around them, farm youngsters found their only playmates and excitement at school.

Even so, going to school often took some getting used to, especially for beginners. Unaccustomed to seeing strangers and painfully shy, many country children found starting school a devastating experience. Herbert Quick, one-time schoolteacher, never forgot the trauma of entering the plain little school in District No. 9, Grundy County, Iowa, with his sister. In *One Man's Life* he told how it was: "Not one of the children spoke to us; they simply sheared off from us and stared. I felt a strange sense of being insulted and humiliated." [Illus. 6.7] This was not Quick's first day in school but his first day in a new school, after his family had moved. For a number of reasons, farm families frequently moved from district to district on the Middle Border, thereby presenting their children with the problem of making friends in new schools. In such circumstances they had to establish their place, and some of the boys did this by foot races or wrestling matches or, as in Quick's case and in Garland's too, by superior scholarly performances that were recognized and admired.

Still, the one-room school—small and humble as it was—was the best kind of school for beginners. It was no huge fortress-like building standing beside a busy street. Its one simple room held no terrors lurking in the corners. It was, in fact, more like an extension of their homes. The little school down the road was already a familiar place to most beginning students. There were few small children in any midwestern school district who had not gone with their parents to meetings of one kind or another at the schoolhouse. Many had visited there with their older brothers and sisters, had enjoyed the attention they received, and could scarcely wait to start school themselves. [Illus. 6.8] Having brothers and sisters and cousins sitting in the same room also helped immensely in easing the transition from home to school.

The midwestern one-room school was really a family school. More often than not its student body was composed of several members of the same family. For example, in the Kebler School in District No. 1, Eagle Township, Eaton County, Michigan, there were five Keblers, five Morrises, two Dotys, three Maloneys, three Thomases, three Allens, and two Hardenburghs

6.9. *All the school-aged children in a family attended the same one-room school. Kebler School, District No. 1, Eagle Township, Eaton County, Michigan. (State Archives of Michigan)*

during the 1890s. [Illus. 6.9] Even without the names, one can tell from the old photographs which children were from the same families merely by observing the clothes they wore. Innumerable boys and girls went off to school clad in dresses and shirts cut from the same bolt of cloth. Their mothers made their clothes from cloth purchased at the general store or ordered by mail and even used the same patterns. [Illus. 6.10]

Besides family relationships, country schoolchildren's clothing also revealed something of the prevailing economic conditions. Consider the children standing before their forlorn log schoolhouse in District No. 19, Frontier County, Nebraska. Some of the girls' dresses and one boy's suit suggest that they dressed in their very best clothes to have their picture taken. But the "very best" of the others—homemade dresses and britches, worn shoes, and wrinkled black stockings—bespeaks their parents' privation, leaving

6.8. *Small children who were too young to enroll frequently became familiar with the school by visiting their sisters and brothers there. Knapp School, Wabaunsee County, Kansas. (KSHS)*

6.10 *The children's clothing revealed family relationships. High Street School, Racine County, Wisconsin. (Whi [X3] 37549, SHSW)*

6.11 *A school district's economic condition was reflected in the clothes the farmers' children wore to school as well as in its schoolhouse. (Seventeenth Biennial Report of the Nebraska Superintendent of Public Instruction, 1901–1902 [Lincoln, 1903], p. 44)*

6.12 *The "Sunday best" clothes the children wore to school to have their picture taken suggest a touch of prosperity in District No. 73. (Seventeenth Biennial Report of the Nebraska Superintendent of Public Instruction, 1901–1902 [Lincoln, 1903], p. 384)*

to the imagination the sacrifices that had to be made merely to have a school in that place. [Illus. 6.11] The photograph showing the attire of the children in Frontier County's District No. 73, taken about the same time, presents a contrast. The parents' ability to provide "Sunday-best" clothes for their children—a middle-class aspiration—hints at a bit of prosperity. [Illus. 6.12] But even the best-dressed children in the one-room schools would probably have been uncomfortable and embarrassed by their clothing in an urban school. The young girls photographed on the propped-up porch of their unpainted Logan County, Kansas, school would undoubtedly have felt completely out of place in their look-alike dresses and bare feet in a village or town school. [Illus. 6.13] Here, however, standing with a certain innate dignity, each with a different pose, they seem unmindful of the poverty of their surroundings and even proud of their dresses, which might have been newly made for this occasion.

Indeed, neither the quantity nor the quality of their clothes seemed important to midwestern country children, if their memoirs are any reflection of their concern. Perhaps this was because the school districts they lived in were so small that great extremes of wealth and poverty rarely existed. To be sure, there were large farmers and small farmers, immigrants and renters, which

accounted for some differences. Even so, one family's children wore just about the same kind of homemade clothes as another's. Midwestern children, then, with the possible exception of newly arrived immigrants, rarely needed to feel ashamed of the clothes they wore to school. Nor did their parents feel compelled to take them out of school because they could not afford nicer clothes.

Unlike those schools requiring children to wear uniforms to provide an artificial kind of democracy, midwestern country schools were the most democratic in the nation—except for their exclusion of blacks. More than any other they fulfilled Horace Mann's dream of schools that were common to all, and the spirit of democracy pervading them was one of their major sources of strength. In such little schools, children generally had a sense of well-being and security, believing that their families were as good as any other in the district. This was especially true of families of old American stock, like Hamlin Garland's. "In all essentials my life was typical of the time and place," he wrote of his boyhood days in Iowa. "My father was counted a good and successful farmer. Our neighbors all lived with the same restricted fashion as ourselves, in barren little houses of wood or stone, owning few books, reading only weekly papers. It was a pure democracy wherein my father was a leader and my

6.13. *Content to have their picture taken at their humble one-room schoolhouse in Logan County, Kansas, the three smallest girls shown here would probably have been uncomfortable in their home-made, look-alike dresses in a city school. (KSHS)*

mother beloved by all who knew her. If anybody looked down upon us, we didn't know it, and in all social affairs of the township we fully shared."

Pure democracy for country schoolchildren, however, ended when the school bell rang and the teacher took charge. First, she assigned the children their seats with little regard for their wishes. In the Victorian years, this often meant

6.14. *Forced to sit with the girls for punishment, one student remembered sitting behind the girl he most admired, whose auburn curls "trailed over the McGuffey page." One-room schoolhouse, Racine, Wisconsin. (Whi [X3] 24590, SHSW)*

that the girls were seated on one side of the class-room and the boys on the other. Decorum seemed to demand it, but the teachers also used this arrangement to discipline unruly boys by forcing them to sit with the girls. In theory, this discipli-nary measure seemed brilliant; in practice, how-ever, it sometimes proved less so. The country school was filled with young loves, and one scholar remembered how he ended up, not unpleasantly, behind the girl who was the object of his youthful admiration. He sat, he wrote, behind his "beloved Martha," whose auburn curls "trailed over the McGuffey page at 'Abhor, annul, construct.' " [Illus. 6.14]

Nor was the school's curriculum at all democ-ratic. It offered few alternatives to the basics. There was no time or money or even an incli-nation to give students choices by adding to the standard curriculum. True, the study of agri-culture was added in some schools in the early 1900s to keep farm children on the farm, but it was by no means universally accepted. The basics, which included the eight common branches of learning—reading, writing, arithme-tic, history, geography, grammar, orthography, and hygiene—were drilled into the students al-most without pause.

During the day, they were called in groups to the teacher's desk to read or recite. When not reciting, they were directed to do slate work at their desks, memorize their lessons, work arith-metic problems, diagram sentences, or draw maps at the blackboard. In between all this there might be trips to the water bucket and to the out-door privies. [Illus. 6.15] The tiny schoolroom fairly hummed with activity, which, with all the coming and going, seemed more chaotic than constructive. Indeed, many remembered the one-room schoolroom as being somewhat noisy, but the noise was usually associated with the learning process, for which the country school provided a more fitting environment than might have been expected.

The gentle rasp of chalk on the blackboard as students added up their sums, the subdued whis-pering of students working together at their big double desks, and the steady drone of the recita-tion going on at the front of the room (or at the back, where the teacher had asked an older stu-

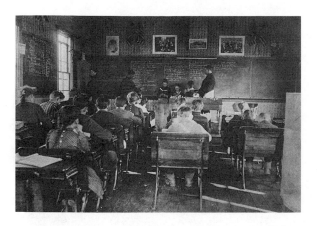

6.15. *In this one-room school in Lauramie Township, Tippecanoe County, Indiana, some students read in front of the class, some worked at the blackboard, and some studied at their seats as the little room hummed with activity. (TCHA Archives)*

EL DORADO, March 2nd.
MRS. HAZELRIGG,
Dear Friend:—I am a little girl nine years of age and go to school and am in the third reader and study arithmetic spelling and writing. My teachers name is Miss Belle Chipps. There are four more weeks of school now, and I have (34) thirty four head marks. Mr. Armstrong (our former teacher) drew a deer and swan last winter on the black board. This winter our teacher and one of the large girls took collored chalk and drew them over and decorated them, we have thirty pupils in roll. We have a very beautiful school house here I am going to speak a piece the last day of school. I like my teacher very much. We have to wreaths with God bless our school and the other is Be good and you will be happy, I live a quarter of a mile from the school house. The school house has got some flags in it. I will close. Your friend
Myrtle Garrison, Liberty, Kan.

6.16. *Midwestern country children kept track of the number of "head marks" they received in spelling bees, as indicated by this letter from a student to the county superintendent. (*Eldorado *Educational Advance, Apr. 1, 1893, p. 4)*

dent to listen to younger ones recite) were the usual sounds of the classroom. And if the younger ones listened to their older brothers' and sisters' recitations, it was no loss. Repetition being a key to learning, their exposure to advanced material paved the way for better understanding when it was thrust upon them. Many, in fact, absorbed so much of the upper-class work that they were able to skip a grade or two.

Skipping grades was not uncommon in the country schools. Unlike in the graded urban schools, there was room for flexibility. If a student fell behind in a subject, he or she might recite with a lower group in that one subject. Or a student who was ahead of the class in a subject might join a more advanced class.

Midwestern country children also learned much through their teachers' competitive methods, which helped prepare them for competition in the outside world. Regularly on Friday afternoons, the schoolroom came alive with cipherdowns and spelling matches. Toeing the mark at the head of the line of students, the first student remained in that position until he or she misspelled a word. When that happened, the student went to the end of the line and started over. The scholar at the head of the line when the contest ended won the "head mark," and many students kept track of and remembered with pride the number of head marks they had won. [Illus. 6.16]

The idea of competition, of getting ahead, of excelling, was also fostered by the maxims of that era—before educational theory deemphasized it. Perhaps not all farm boys and girls were inspired by such epigrams as "LIVE TO LEARN—STRIVE TO EXCEL" written on the blackboards of their small schoolrooms, but no doubt many were. [Illus. 6.17] And if the hundreds of midwestern country schools that had chosen "UPWARD AND ONWARD" as their motto were

6.17. *The maxim on the blackboard of this schoolroom, "live to learn—strive to excel," like many similar exhortations, inspired rural children to compete, to be ambitious, and to rise above their condition. Arbor Vitae School, Subdistrict No. 7, Oneida Township, Delaware County, Iowa. (SHSI, Iowa City, Huftalen Collection)*

any indication of their students' zeal to struggle, to compete, and to improve their lives, then the children of the Middle West who had ambitions of rising above their stations in life were legion. [Illus. 6.18]

As they advanced from year to year, midwestern country children were exposed to all of the eight common branches of learning, including hygiene—or physiology, as a young student near Eldorado, Kansas, called it in her letter to the county superintendent. [Illus. 6.19] In hygiene class, many students memorized the bones of the body and studied the circulation of the blood. Most were taught health through cleanliness, and above all else they were taught the evil effects of alcohol on the body, which teachers were required to emphasize.

In Monteith's *Manual of Geography*, they studied the boundaries of the states and memorized their capitals, the names and locations of the world's great rivers, the continents, and a host of definitions. An island, they read and

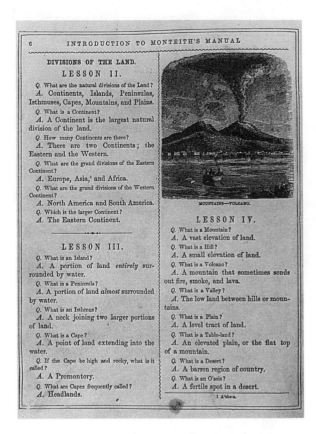

6.20. *From the Introduction to the* Manual of Geography *by James Monteith, thousands of midwestern farm children learned about the earth and the world they lived in by memorizing assorted geographical definitions and place names.*

Left: 6.18. Youthful ambitions were reflected by the motto "UPWARD AND ONWARD," chosen in hundreds of midwestern one-room schools. District No. 1, Clam Lake Township, Wexford County, Michigan. (Sixty-first Annual Report of the Superintendent of Public Instruction of the State of Michigan, 1897 [Lansing, 1898], p. 42)
Right: 6.19. Country students studied the eight common branches of learning. Based on this letter written to the county superintendent, one can only speculate about the grade this student eventually received in grammar. (Eldorado Educational Advance, May 1, 1893, p. 4)

remembered, is "a portion of land *entirely* surrounded by water." [Illus. 6.20]

Nearly all those who wrote of their experiences remembered Ray's *Arithmetic*, perhaps because arithmetic was frequently their favorite subject. In that one book they would go from the simplest numbers to geometrical proportions, mensuration, and the rule of three. "It was a great joy to me," one man recalled, "when I came to the realization that I could solve every problem in Ray's Third Part, including the 'one hundred promiscuous questions.' " [Illus. 6.21]

But it was their readers that country children remembered best as they looked back at their school days—especially *McGuffey's Readers*. First compiled in the 1830s by William McGuffey, a Presbyterian minister in Ohio, they reflected the Puritan-Protestant revival and reform movement that was then sweeping the country.

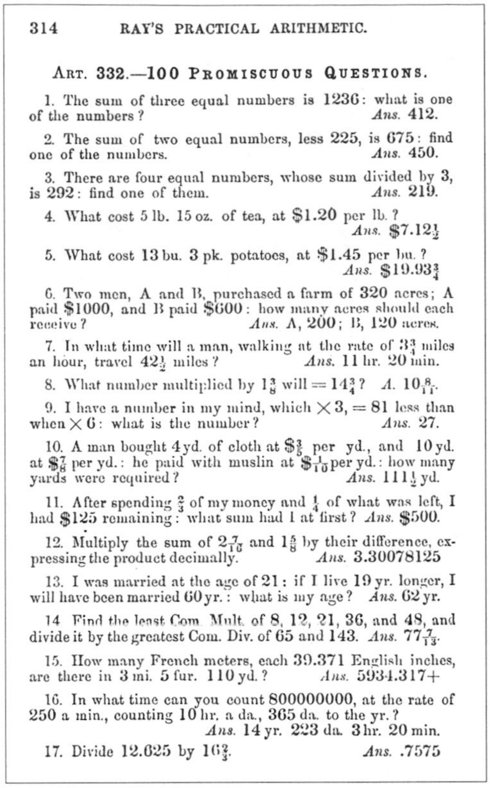

314 RAY'S PRACTICAL ARITHMETIC.

ART. 332.—100 PROMISCUOUS QUESTIONS.

1. The sum of three equal numbers is 1236: what is one of the numbers? *Ans.* 412.

2. The sum of two equal numbers, less 225, is 675: find one of the numbers. *Ans.* 450.

3. There are four equal numbers, whose sum divided by 3, is 292: find one of them. *Ans.* 219.

4. What cost 5 lb. 15 oz. of tea, at \$1.20 per lb.? *Ans.* \$7.12$\frac{1}{2}$

5. What cost 13 bu. 3 pk. potatoes, at \$1.45 per bu.? *Ans.* \$19.93$\frac{3}{4}$

6. Two men, A and B, purchased a farm of 320 acres; A paid \$1000, and B paid \$600: how many acres should each receive? *Ans.* A, 200; B, 120 acres.

7. In what time will a man, walking at the rate of 3$\frac{3}{4}$ miles an hour, travel 42$\frac{1}{2}$ miles? *Ans.* 11 hr. 20 min.

8. What number multiplied by 1$\frac{3}{8}$ will = 14$\frac{3}{4}$? *A.* 10$\frac{8}{11}$.

9. I have a number in my mind, which × 3, = 81 less than when × 6: what is the number? *Ans.* 27.

10. A man bought 4 yd. of cloth at \$$\frac{3}{5}$ per yd., and 10 yd. at \$$\frac{7}{8}$ per yd.: he paid with muslin at \$$\frac{1}{10}$ per yd.: how many yards were required? *Ans.* 111$\frac{1}{2}$ yd.

11. After spending $\frac{2}{3}$ of my money and $\frac{1}{4}$ of what was left, I had \$125 remaining: what sum had I at first? *Ans.* \$500.

12. Multiply the sum of 2$\frac{7}{10}$ and 1$\frac{5}{8}$ by their difference, expressing the product decimally. *Ans.* 3.30078125

13. I was married at the age of 21: if I live 19 yr. longer, I will have been married 60 yr.: what is my age? *Ans.* 62 yr.

14. Find the least Com. Mult. of 8, 12, 21, 36, and 48, and divide it by the greatest Com. Div. of 65 and 143. *Ans.* 77$\frac{7}{13}$.

15. How many French meters, each 39.371 English inches, are there in 3 mi. 5 fur. 110 yd.? *Ans.* 5934.317+

16. In what time can you count 800000000, at the rate of 250 a min., counting 10 hr. a da., 365 da. to the yr.? *Ans.* 14 yr. 223 da. 3 hr. 20 min.

17. Divide 12.625 by 16$\frac{2}{3}$. *Ans.* .7575

6.21. Ray's Arithmetic, Third Book, *was especially popular among midwestern country schools. One student remembered being able to answer all 100 of Ray's promiscuous questions correctly.*

From that time into the early twentieth century, *McGuffey's Readers* and their many imitators were the mainstays of country school education in the Middle West. [Illus. 6.22] Composed of the first through sixth eclectic readers, the books began with the alphabet and simple stories and advanced to excerpts from Shakespeare, the Bible, the best of the English and American poets, biographical sketches of great men, and portions of their orations. Indeed, *McGuffey's Readers* provided a smattering of the most significant persons and literature in Western civilization; neither Alexander the Great nor Socrates, Hamlet nor Lochinvar, was unfamiliar to former students when they ran across them in later years.

Many of the poems they found in the readers they committed to memory and recited in front of their classmates or before proud parents who had gathered at the schoolhouse for a school program. Because the poems rhymed and sketched familiar scenes, they were usually quite easy for the young students to memorize. To children reared on midwestern farms, Longfellow's "Village Blacksmith" was no stranger; and when they came to James Whitcomb Riley's "When the frost is on the pumpkin and the fodder's in the shock," they had only to look at the fields surrounding their schoolhouse to see those shocks, to feel fall in the air, and to understand what the poet was saying. [Illus. 6.23]

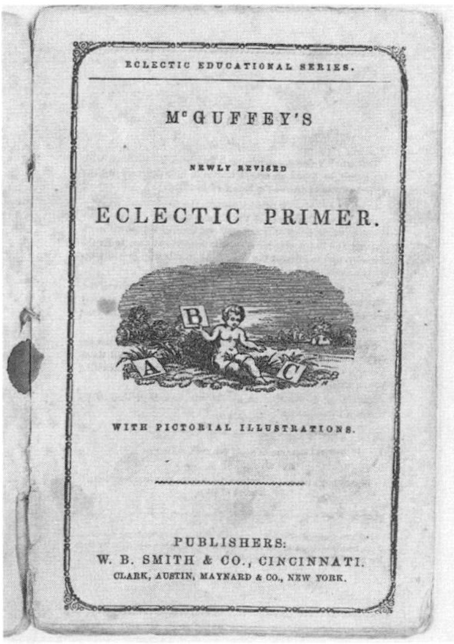

ECLECTIC EDUCATIONAL SERIES.

McGUFFEY'S

NEWLY REVISED

ECLECTIC PRIMER.

WITH PICTORIAL ILLUSTRATIONS.

PUBLISHERS:
W. B. SMITH & CO., CINCINNATI.
CLARK, AUSTIN, MAYNARD & CO., NEW YORK.

6.22. *For more than three-quarters of a century,* McGuffey's Readers *were the standard for midwestern country schools.*

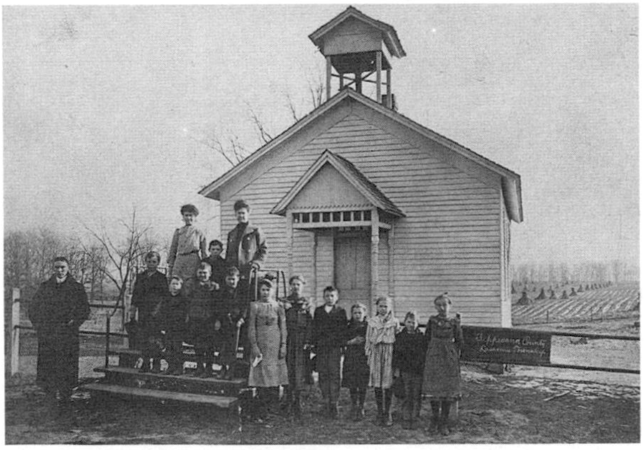

6.23. *James Whitcomb Riley's poem was understandable to country children, who could see the "fodder in the shock" behind this schoolhouse in Lauramie Township, Tippecanoe County, Indiana. (TCHA Archives)*

6.24. *"What I Live For" in* McGuffey's Fifth Eclectic Reader *emphasized life's moral purpose.* (McGuffey's Fifth Eclectic Reader, *rev. ed. [New York: Van Nostrand Reinhold, 1879], p. 91)*

XXIV. WHAT I LIVE FOR.

1. I LIVE for those who love me,
    Whose hearts are kind and true;
   For the heaven that smiles above me,
    And awaits my spirit, too;
   For all human ties that bind me,
    For the task my God assigned me,
    For the bright hopes left behind me,
    And the good that I can do.

2. I live to learn their story,
    Who suffered for my sake;
   To emulate their glory,
    And follow in their wake;
   Bards, patriots, martyrs, sages,
   The noble of all ages,
   Whose deeds crown History's pages,
    And Time's great volume make.

6.26. *Maxims of moral uplift on the walls and blackboards of most midwestern one-room schools urged students to persevere.* District No. 5, Colfax Township, Huron County, Michigan. *(Sixty-first Annual Report of the Superintendent of Public Instruction of the State of Michigan, 1897 [Lansing, 1898], p. 67)*

The orations of great men reproduced in their readers were especially appealing to midwestern farm boys of the late nineteenth century. For many of them, oratory was a passion. Imagining themselves swaying great audiences with the power of their rhetoric, they recited Webster's second reply to Hayne, Regulus to the Carthaginians, Patrick Henry to the Virginia convention, and many others as they drove cows from the pasture or plowed a field or walked to school.

The readers were more than anthologies of great literary and historical works, however. They were intended to inspire children with noble goals and give them a purpose in life. "What I Live For," found in *McGuffey's Fifth Eclectic Reader*, explains much about the mindset of the books and of the young people who read them. [Illus. 6.24] Along with lofty goals, the readers were designed to indoctrinate the children with nineteenth-century moral lessons they never forgot.

About moral values and their place in education there was no confusion in midwestern

one-room schools. They were largely Protestant-Puritan values, drawn from the Old and New Testaments, the Ten Commandments, and the Sermon on the Mount. These values were as readily accepted by most midwesterners as democracy, with which they were closely allied. From their first day in school, country children were surrounded by moral lessons. Commonly the school day began with prayer, the reading of the Bible, the singing of a hymn, or all three. Only occasionally were objections raised to such practices, but when they were, the battle cries reverberated around the region.

For years, Daniel Freeman—sometimes called the nation's first homesteader—had been able to keep the teacher from including these religious exercises in the school that bore his name in District No. 21, Gage County, Nebraska. But then Edith Beacher, a Baptist, became the teacher there. She regarded religious instruction as part of her duty and read the Bible and prayed in defiance of Freeman. He once rode into the school yard to threaten her. [Illus. 6.25]. Blocked by the teacher's obstinacy and unable to secure support from the state superintendent of public instruction, Freeman resorted to the courts to force the teacher to forgo Bible reading and prayer. Rejected by the Gage County District Court, the suit was appealed to the state Supreme Court, which ordered an end to such activities. Nevertheless, the local paper carried the story under

6.25 *In the early 1900s, Daniel Freeman, the first homesteader, rode into this school yard to demand that the teacher stop praying and reading the Bible in class.* Freeman School, District No. 21, Gage County, Nebraska.

6.27. *Lofty moral instruction sometimes appeared even in the naming of one-room schools. This is the Know Thyself School in District No. 11, Greenwood County, Kansas. (KSHS)*

6.28. *The value of punctuality was reinforced by inscriptions on the schoolroom walls. District No. 8, Berrien Township, Berrien County, Michigan. (Sixty-first Annual Report of the Superintendent of Public Instruction of the State of Michigan, 1897 [Lansing, 1898], p. 50)*

the headline "IGNORE THE COURT"—advice that was surely followed in thousands of little schools throughout Nebraska and across the Middle West. But whether in-school prayers or Bible reading continued, the teaching of moral principles—emphasized by both educators and parents—remained, in one way or another, as much a part of the school curriculum as the three Rs.

The children's country schoolrooms were shrouded with the century's aphorisms of uplift. Day after day they sat looking at such chalk-printed adages as "TRY TRY TRY," "DO YOUR BEST," and "BE KIND AND COURTEOUS," which lined the walls of their schoolrooms. [Illus. 6.26] Sometimes even the name of the school suggested the moral nature of their instruction. The school in District No. 11 in Greenwood County, Kansas, was called "Know Thyself," a name probably drawn from a snippet of Alexander Pope's *Essay on Man* contained in a reader. [Illus. 6.27]

From the lessons in their readers, students learned of the dangers of waste, the rewards of honesty, and the virtues of punctuality, reinforced occasionally by a reminder on the blackboard or the schoolroom wall. [Illus. 6.28] They also discovered the value of courage, patience, and persistence and the sin of idleness in *McGuffey's Readers*. Many never forgot the story of Hugh Idle and Mr. Toil in the fourth reader, and one student who became a prominent educator claimed that the poem "Harry and the Guidepost" in the third reader stayed with him all his life. [Illus. 6.29]

Much history, too, could be taught from the readers, for they were filled with biographical sketches of great men, stories of famous battles, and historical scenes such as the landing of the Pilgrims. In the Middle West's one-room schools, no more confusion existed about the teaching of history than about the teaching of morality. The greatness of the nation was the theme of the history taught there, and the development of patriotism was its purpose. To supplement the patriotic selections in the readers, patriotic ceremonies in the school yard signaled the beginning

6.29. *The guidepost shrouded in gloom taught a valuable lesson. (McGuffey's Third Eclectic Reader, rev. ed. [New York: Van Nostrand Reinhold, 1879], p. 122)*

6.30. *The nation's greatness was taught in country schools in order to develop patriotism. Children and teachers proudly pledged allegiance to the flag each day, as at the Cabell School in Logan County, Kansas (left) and the Solomon Valley School in Graham County, Kansas (right). (KSHS)*

6.32. *Country children were heirs to the great outdoors. At the Deckard School in Brown County, Indiana, the countryside—with its natural, unplanned attractions—beckoned to them at noon and recess in ways that urban children would find strange. (Ind. Univ. Foundation)*

of school each morning. In the 1890s, flagpoles sprouted in country school yards like buds on the trees in springtime, and midwestern children gathered around them to raise the flag and pledge their allegiance to it. Different ways of saluting the flag were inconsequential; it was the sentiment that mattered. [Illus. 6.30]

Perhaps it was easier to teach country children in one-room schoolhouses of the Middle West about the greatness of their country than it is to teach it to those in urban centers today. For them, the past was not so far past, and somehow

6.31. *The portraits of the father and the savior of the nation looked down from the walls of countless midwestern country schoolrooms, and few children did not know which was which. Fox Den School, District No. 12, Wabash Township, Tippecanoe County, Indiana. (TCHA Archives)*

there was less to be confused about. The cataclysmic Civil War shadowed all their lives. Every community had its veterans of that war, and their influence on the lives of the young children can never be measured. As they listened in awe to veterans tell their stories of the conflict and watched them parade in their uniforms on Memorial Day, they pictured in their minds and never forgot the far-away battle scenes they had heard about.

To add to that, a sense of the past haunted the little schoolrooms. The nation's flag hung in front of the rooms, replicas of historical documents were scattered about, and portraits of Washington and Lincoln, often secured from the Perry set, looked down from the walls of countless schoolrooms. The children were reminded daily of both the father and the savior of their country, and few, if any, in that broad region left school not knowing which was which. [Illus. 6.31] Of course, it was easy for them to identify with these heroes of the Republic. It was not so very far from the rural life of Washington's plantation to life on a midwestern farm. And Lincoln's life in Indiana and Illinois was no distance at all.

Like Lincoln and Washington, children of the rural Middle West were heirs of the great outdoors. Farm chores and farm work, trips to

6.33. *In winter, when the school yard lay bathed in snow, midwestern children would slide down white-clad hills or skate on a nearby creek that had frozen. Green Valley School, Brown County, Indiana. (Ind. Univ. Foundation)*

6.34. *Remembering battles they had read about, schoolboys built forts in the snow during the noon hour and bombarded their enemies with snowballs at the Oak Grove School in Shawnee County, Kansas. (KSHS)*

church and occasional trips to town, and the walk back and forth to school forced them to spend many of their waking hours in the open air. Even at school, the rugged, unplanned outdoors that beckoned to them at recess and noontime was completely different from the structured outdoor environment of urban children. Their experiences on the school grounds were a vital part of what they learned at school. [Illus. 6.32]

Until the aftermath of the First World War, country school yards were usually as bereft of playground equipment as they were of trees, but this was of little consequence to farm children. Inventing their own amusements or adapting old hand-me-down games to their uses, they competed as fiercely with one another as they did in the classroom and learned—not always painlessly—about winning and losing and how they fit into the scheme of things. In winter, when snow covered the school yard and surrounding area, they slid down powdery hills, skated on the frozen creek, or played fox-and-geese in circles that covered the whole schoolyard. [Illus. 6.33] Sometimes, imagining themselves in battles they had read about, they built forts in the snow, chose up sides, and bombarded each other's positions with shells of snow. [Illus. 6.34]

In warmer weather, they opted for games familiar to schoolchildren everywhere. They ran races and played dare-base, tag, and that all-time favorite, hide-and-seek. [Illus. 6.35] The girls could spend all recess and even the noon hour catching one another in London-Bridge-is-falling-down or running the circle in ring-around-the-rosy; the boys who were fortunate enough to have the equipment played ball. That they did not have enough students to make two teams was of little consequence. They improvised as they went along, adapting their game to whatever numbers they could muster. [Illus. 6.36]

6.35. *Not many games were more popular in country school yards than hide-and-seek. (OHS)*

6.36. *The lack of playground equipment led country children to play games handed down from generation to generation and to develop some of their own. (Whi [W6] 3285, SHSW)*

6.38. *Unfenced school yards made the surrounding fields and prairies an inviting and irresistible playground for rural children. McStay School, Osborne County, Kansas. (KSHS)*

At the noon hour, they hurried to the cloakroom to retrieve their lunch pails, which were packed with meat, fruit, and vegetables that had been grown and prepared on their own farms. [Illus. 6.37] On very cold days, they sometimes found their food frozen and thawed it out on the big stove. On such days they ate their lunches in the classroom, but when the weather was nice, lunches were hurriedly eaten outdoors. This left time, especially for the boys, to race through the

6.37. *Children's lunches were packed with food grown and prepared at home and were eaten in the warmth of the schoolhouse on winter days. (SHSI, Iowa City, E. M. Clark Collection)*

unfenced school yards to the fields and woods that lay open to their wandering. On the prairies they dug for gophers, built forts, and acted out whatever scenarios their active imaginations could devise until the bell rang, summoning them back to their studies. [Illus. 6.38]

For all the fun of school games in the outdoors, however, it was hard to surpass the last day of school, when parents and grandparents gathered at the schoolhouse for the school picnic and program. While parents visited with one another, the children played games until noon. Then everyone circled a makeshift table, loaded their plates with food, and settled down to eat. When the picnic was over, children and adults trooped into the schoolhouse, where proud parents watched their children sing or speak pieces or deliver orations or participate in a spell-down. [Illus. 6.39]

The average school year on the Middle Border was about eight months in 1900. But this did not mean that all children attended for the entire school term. The attendance of older children, especially older boys, was usually sporadic, because they were needed to help on the farm. The result was that many of them dropped out of school by their teens. Yet a surprisingly large number continued to attend sporadically. The flexibility of classes—loosely organized into three general grades—made it possible for them

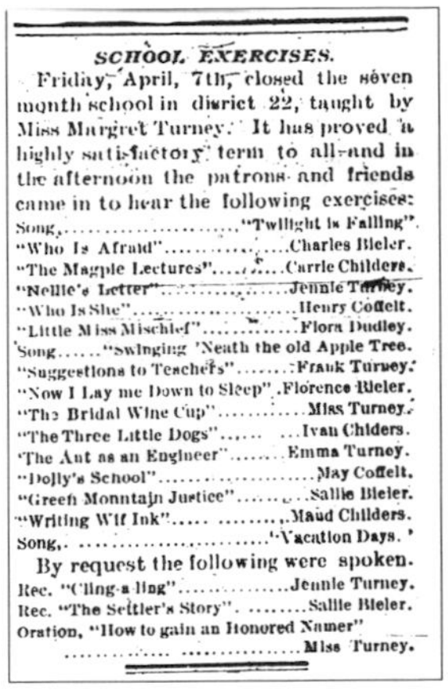

SCHOOL EXERCISES.

Friday, April, 7th, closed the seven month school in disrict 22, taught by Miss Margret Turney. It has proved a highly satisfactory term to all—and in the afternoon the patrons and friends came in to hear the following exercises:

Song,........................"Twilight is Falling".
"Who Is Afraid"................Charles Bieler.
"The Magpie Lectures"..........Carrie Childers.
"Nellie's Letter"..............Jennie Turney.
"Who Is She"...................Henry Coffelt.
"Little Miss Mischief".........Flora Dudley.
Song......"Swinging 'Neath the old Apple Tree.
"Suggestions to Teachers"........Frank Turney.
"Now I Lay me Down to Sleep". Florence Bieler.
"The Bridal Wine Cup"...........Miss Turney.
"The Three Little Dogs".........Ivan Childers.
"The Ant as an Engineer"........Emma Turney.
"Dolly's School"...................May Coffelt.
"Green Mountain Justice"........Sallie Bieler.
"Writing Wif Ink"...............Maud Childers.
Song,.............................."Vacation Days."

By request the following were spoken.

Rec. "Cling-a-ling"................Jennie Turney.
Rec. "The Settler's Story"..........Sallie Bieler.
Oration, "How to gain an Honored Name"
....Miss Turney.

6.39. The last day of school often ended with a picnic and always with a program for parents and grandparents. (Eldorado Educational Advance, *May 1, 1893, p. 6)*

to drop out and reenter without the embarrassment of being assigned to a beginning class. Long before educators devised the slogan of "take the student where he is," country schools had been practicing it successfully for years.

By the early 1900s, however, a large percentage of the Midwest's one-room schools had been graded, and students were passed from grade to grade until they graduated from the eighth grade. To reach this much-sought-after distinction, they had to pass countywide examinations similar to that shown in Illus. 6.40. Obviously, these examinations reflected what eighth graders were expected to know, which was no small body of knowledge. Many of the questions asked would have been difficult for today's high school graduate to answer, and passing the test required more than simply being present.

Late on an autumn afternoon in 1897, after the school day had officially ended, the Michigan state superintendent came upon the schoolhouse in District No. 3, Monitor Township, Bay County. It was a large, well-furnished schoolhouse—capable of seating eighty students—with a commodious entry and alcove. To his surprise, he found eighteen eighth-grade students still at work, diagramming sentences, solving algebraic and arithmetical problems on the blackboard, and asking their teacher for further instructions. When asked about this, the teacher replied that it was the custom for this class to linger for additional work until five o'clock. [Illus. 6.41]

Although this was unusual, it is fair to say that some such effort was required of all the children who hoped to pass the stringent county examina-

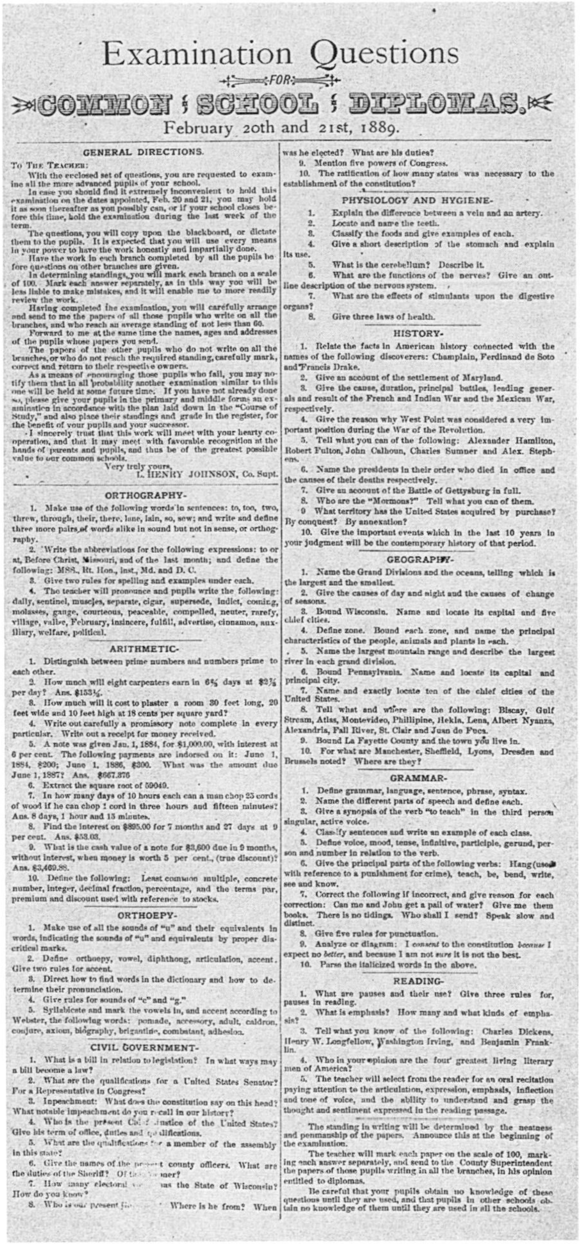

Examination Questions

FOR

COMMON SCHOOL DIPLOMAS.

February 20th and 21st, 1889.

GENERAL DIRECTIONS.

To The Teacher:

With the enclosed set of questions, you are requested to examine all the more advanced pupils of your school.

In case you should find it extremely inconvenient to hold this examination on the dates appointed, Feb. 20 and 21, you may hold it as soon thereafter as you possibly can, or if your school closes before this time, hold the examination during the last week of the term.

The questions, you will copy upon the blackboard, or dictate them to the pupils. It is expected that you will use every means in your power to have the work honestly and impartially done.

Have the work in each branch completed by all the pupils before questions on other branches are given.

In determining standings, you will mark each branch on a scale of 100. Mark each answer separately, as in this way you will be less liable to make mistakes, and it will enable me to more readily review the work.

Having completed the examination, you will carefully arrange and send to me the papers of all those pupils who write on all the branches, and who reach an average standing of not less than 60.

Forward to me at the same time the names, ages and addresses of the pupils whose papers you send.

The papers of the other pupils who do not write on all the branches, or who do not reach the required standing, carefully mark, correct and return to their respective owners.

As a means of encouraging those pupils who fail, you may notify them that in all probability another examination similar to this one will be held at some future time. If you have not already done so, please give your pupils in the primary and middle forms an examination in accordance with the plan laid down in the "Course of Study," and also place their standings and grade in the register, for the benefit of your pupils and your successor.

I sincerely trust that this work will meet with your hearty co-operation, and that it may meet with favorable recognition at the hands of parents and pupils, and thus be of the greatest possible value to our common schools.

Very truly yours,
L. HENRY JOHNSON, Co. Supt.

ORTHOGRAPHY-

1. Make use of the following words in sentences: to, too, two, threw, through, their, there, lane, lain, so, sew; and write and define three more pairs of words alike in sound but not in sense, or orthography.
2. Write the abbreviations for the following expressions: to or at, Before Christ, Missouri, and of the last month; and define the following: MSS., Rt. Hon., inst., Md. and D. C.
3. Give two rules for spelling and examples under each.
4. The teacher will pronounce and pupils write the following: daily, sentinel, muscles, separate, cigar, supersede, indict, coming, molasses, gauge, courteous, peaceable, compelled, neuter, rarefy, village, valise, February, insincere, fulfill, advertise, cinnamon, auxiliary, welfare, political.

ARITHMETIC-

1. Distinguish between prime numbers and numbers prime to each other.
2. How much will eight carpenters earn in 6⅘ days at \$2⅚ per day? Ans. \$153⅓.
3. How much will it cost to plaster a room 30 feet long, 20 feet wide and 10 feet high at 18 cents per square yard?
4. Write out carefully a promissory note complete in every particular. Write out a receipt for money received.
5. A note was given Jan. 1, 1884, for \$1,000.00, with interest at 6 per cent. The following payments are indorsed on it: June 1, 1884, \$200; June 1, 1886, \$300. What was the amount due June 1, 1887? Ans. \$667.376
6. Extract the square root of 59049.
7. In how many days of 10 hours each can a man chop 25 cords of wood if he can chop 1 cord in three hours and fifteen minutes? Ans. 8 days, 1 hour and 15 minutes.
8. Find the interest on \$895.00 for 7 months and 27 days at 9 per cent. Ans. \$53.03.
9. What is the cash value of a note for \$3,600 due in 9 months, without interest, when money is worth 5 per cent., (true discount)? Ans. \$3,469.88.
10. Define the following: Least common multiple, concrete number, integer, decimal fraction, percentage, and the terms par, premium and discount used with reference to stocks.

ORTHOEPY-

1. Make use of all the sounds of "u" and their equivalents in words, indicating the sounds of "u" and equivalents by proper diacritical marks.
2. Define orthoepy, vowel, diphthong, articulation, accent. Give two rules for accent.
3. Direct how to find words in the dictionary and how to determine their pronunciation.
4. Give rules for sounds of "c" and "g."
5. Syllabicate and mark the vowels in, and accent according to Webster, the following words: pomade, accessory, adult, caldron, conjure, axiom, biography, brigantine, combatant, adhesion.

CIVIL GOVERNMENT-

1. What is a bill in relation to legislation? In what ways may a bill become a law?
2. What are the qualifications for a United States Senator? For a Representative in Congress?
3. Impeachment: What does the constitution say on this head? What notable impeachment do you recall in our history?
4. Who is the present Chief Justice of the United States? Give his term of office, duties and qualifications.
5. What are the qualifications for a member of the assembly in this state?
6. Give the names of the present county officers. What are the duties of the Sheriff? Of the [illegible]ner?
7. How many electoral [illegible] has the State of Wisconsin? How do you know?
8. Who is our present [illegible] Where is he from? When was he elected? What are his duties?
9. Mention five powers of Congress.
10. The ratification of how many states was necessary to the establishment of the constitution?

PHYSIOLOGY AND HYGIENE-

1. Explain the difference between a vein and an artery.
2. Locate and name the teeth.
3. Classify the foods and give examples of each.
4. Give a short description of the stomach and explain its use.
5. What is the cerebellum? Describe it.
6. What are the functions of the nerves? Give an outline description of the nervous system.
7. What are the effects of stimulants upon the digestive organs?
8. Give three laws of health.

HISTORY-

1. Relate the facts in American history connected with the names of the following discoverers: Champlain, Ferdinand de Soto and Francis Drake.
2. Give an account of the settlement of Maryland.
3. Give the cause, duration, principal battles, leading generals and result of the French and Indian War and the Mexican War, respectively.
4. Give the reason why West Point was considered a very important position during the War of the Revolution.
5. Tell what you can of the following: Alexander Hamilton, Robert Fulton, John Calhoun, Charles Sumner and Alex. Stephens.
6. Name the presidents in their order who died in office and the causes of their deaths respectively.
7. Give an account of the Battle of Gettysburg in full.
8. Who are the "Mormons?" Tell what you can of them.
9. What territory has the United States acquired by purchase? By conquest? By annexation?
10. Give the important events which in the last 10 years in your judgment will be the contemporary history of that period.

GEOGRAPHY-

1. Name the Grand Divisions and the oceans, telling which is the largest and the smallest.
2. Give the causes of day and night and the causes of change of seasons.
3. Bound Wisconsin. Name and locate its capital and five chief cities.
4. Define zone. Bound each zone, and name the principal characteristics of the people, animals and plants in each.
5. Name the largest mountain range and describe the largest river in each grand division.
6. Bound Pennsylvania. Name and locate its capital and principal city.
7. Name and exactly locate ten of the chief cities of the United States.
8. Tell what and where are the following: Biscay, Gulf Stream, Atlas, Montevideo, Phillipine, Hekla, Lena, Albert Nyanza, Alexandria, Fall River, St. Clair and Juan de Fuca.
9. Bound La Fayette County and the town you live in.
10. For what are Manchester, Sheffield, Lyons, Dresden and Brussels noted? Where are they?

GRAMMAR-

1. Define grammar, language, sentence, phrase, syntax.
2. Name the different parts of speech and define each.
3. Give a synopsis of the verb "to teach" in the third person singular, active voice.
4. Classify sentences and write an example of each class.
5. Define voice, mood, tense, infinitive, participle, gerund, person and number in relation to the verb.
6. Give the principal parts of the following verbs: Hang (used with reference to a punishment for crime), teach, be, bend, write, see and know.
7. Correct the following if incorrect, and give reason for each correction: Can me and John get a pail of water? Give me them books. There is no tidings. Who shall I send? Speak slow and distinct.
8. Give five rules for punctuation.
9. Analyze or diagram: I *consent* to the constitution *because* I expect no *better*, and because I am not *sure* it is not the best.
10. Parse the italicized words in the above.

READING-

1. What are pauses and their use? Give three rules for, pauses in reading.
2. What is emphasis? How many and what kinds of emphasis?
3. Tell what you know of the following: Charles Dickens, Henry W. Longfellow, Washington Irving, and Benjamin Franklin.
4. Who in your opinion are the four greatest living literary men of America?
5. The teacher will select from the reader for an oral recitation paying attention to the articulation, expression, emphasis, inflection and tone of voice, and the ability to understand and grasp the thought and sentiment expressed in the reading passage.

The standing in writing will be determined by the neatness and penmanship of the papers. Announce this at the beginning of the examination.

The teacher will mark each paper on the scale of 100, marking each answer separately, and send to the County Superintendent the papers of those pupils writing in all the branches, in his opinion entitled to diplomas.

Be careful that your pupils obtain no knowledge of these questions until they are used, and that pupils in other schools obtain no knowledge of them until they are used in all the schools.

6.40. To graduate from the eighth grade, students had to pass a rigorous countywide examination of the kind shown here. (Whi [X3] 43029, SHSW)

tions. And, of course, many did not pass. But those who did gathered in the spring of the year at the county seat, where they were given diplomas in special graduation ceremonies. [Illus. 6.42] Graduation from the eighth grade was the glorious culmination of country school education in the Middle West. Looking back on her own graduation ceremony, a Kansas woman

6.41. *The eighth-grade class in this Michigan school-house was accustomed to staying after school to diagram sentences and work algebraic problems. The white banner contains the class roll. (Sixty-first Annual Report of the Superintendent of Public Instruction of the State of Michigan, 1897 [Lansing, 1898], p. 48)*

6.42. *Country school students throughout the Middle Border received their eighth-grade diplomas in countywide graduation ceremonies at the county seat. York County, Nebraska, eighth-grade graduates, 1902. (Eighteenth Biennial Report of the Nebraska State Superintendent of Public Instruction, 1903–1905 [Lincoln, 1905], p. 359)*

6.43. *For the eighth-grade graduation ceremonies at the county seat, these scholars from Page County, Iowa, dressed in their finest clothes. (SHSI, Iowa City, Huftalen Collection)*

6.44. *Many of the students in this high school in St. John, Clinton County, Michigan, were graduates of the county's one-room schools, which, according to the state superintendent, compared "favorably with the eight grades of Lansing or St. John's." (Sixty-first Annual Report of the Superintendent of Public Instruction of the State of Michigan, 1897 [Lansing, 1898], frontispiece)*

wrote: "When my family took me on an overnight trip to the county seat, the evening ceremony of diploma-bestowal seemed to me a blaze of lights and glory." And so it was for many country boys and girls, who seldom ventured much beyond their little communities. It was a time to dress up in their Sunday best, to bask in the glory of their achievement, and to have their pictures taken. [Illus. 6.43]

From the last years of the nineteenth century to as long as the country schools lasted, an eighth-grade diploma was the country student's ticket to the nearest high school, and many made that journey. Often the best-prepared students in the high school, most of them did well academically, and many went on to become the teachers, lawyers, physicians, and political leaders of their communities and states. Of the fifty-eight students in the high school in St. John, Michigan, in 1897, many were graduates of Clinton County's country schools, and all were from rural homes. [Illus. 6.44] They had been taught, according to the Michigan state superintendent, by country-born teachers who had no professional training except that given in the teacher institutes. In short, they were the products of the area's one-room schools, and their training had turned out to be as good as that received by those educated in town and village schools. "The eight grades of the country schools of Clinton County," the state superintendent wrote, "compare very favorably with the eight grades of Lansing or St. John's. In large measure, this achievement was attributable to those earnest teachers who had so little professional training but more than a little common sense.

Chapter 7

Teacher! Teacher!

7.1. *In the 1870s, mid-western farmers usually ordered their school boards to employ male teachers for the winter term. (Minutes, Jt. Dist. No. 1, Koshkonong, Whitewater, Cold Springs, and Lima Twps., Jefferson Co., Wis., School Records, SHSW)*

"The teacher made the school," midwesterners used to say, and of course it was true. At least it was so in the area's one-room schools, where the expression probably originated. It was not the parents, important as they were, or the school board, and certainly not the one-room schoolhouse that made a good school. In the end, no school, no matter how well equipped, was better than its teacher.

In the twilight years of the old century and the beginning of the new, the midwestern country schoolteacher was part of a small army pushing back the barriers of ignorance across the heartland. At the end of World War I, almost 160,000 of them were teaching in the region's rural schools. [Table 7.1] Once, shortly after the Civil War, nearly half of all schoolteachers in the Midwest had been men, and for years, male teachers were much preferred over female. In the 1870s, and even into the next decade, farmers in thousands of districts instructed their school boards at every annual meeting to employ a male teacher at least for the winter term, when the older boys were in school. [Illus. 7.1] But by 1900, the total number of male teachers in the common schools had dwindled to 29 percent of the total; seven-

Table 7.1. Midwestern Rural Teachers, 1918

State	Men	Women	% Male
Illinois	3,281	14,860	18.1
Indiana	5,317	4,728	52.9
Iowa	1,995	20,349	8.9
Kansas	2,027	11,087	15.5
Michigan	2,049	11,430	15.2
Minnesota	1,291	12,353	9.5
Missouri	3,361	10,587	24.1
Nebraska	505	10,074	4.8
North Dakota	715	5,985	10.7
Ohio	5,323	12,962	29.1
South Dakota	686	6,044	10.2
Wisconsin	1,079	10,196	9.6
T O T A L	27,629	130,655	17.4

S O U R C E : U.S. Bureau of Education, 1919, Bulletin No. 90, Vol. 3 (Washington, D.C.: GPO, 1919), p. 30.

Table 7.2. Teachers' Salaries, 1901

State	Male	Female
Illinois	$61.69	$53.51
Indiana	63.40	42.40
Iowa	41.53	30.68
Kansas	42.90	35.85
Michigan	48.60	36.54
Minnesota	44.80	36.45
Missouri [a]	49.50	42.50
Nebraska	47.54	38.23
North Dakota [b]	41.72	36.80
Ohio	40.00	35.00
South Dakota	34.70	31.17
Wisconsin	53.33	38.52

S O U R C E : *Report of the Commissioner of Education, 1901* (Washington, D.C.: GPO, 1902), p. lxxxv.
[a] Figures are for 1897–98.
[b] Figures are for 1899–1900.

teen years later, only 17.4 percent of all rural teachers were men (see Table 7.1). By that time, country schoolteaching had long since become women's work in the midwestern mind.

In times past, female teachers had been thought incapable of handling large farm boys who towered above them. For years, they were hired only to teach the young children during the spring and summer terms. But as the frontier receded and community life stabilized, many school directors and their constituents became convinced that women could be even better country schoolteachers than men. Besides, women taught for a much lower monthly salary than men, which was too good a bargain for frugal farmers to pass up. [Table 7.2]

But the farmers' desire to employ the cheapest teachers was not the only reason—or perhaps even the principal reason—for the predominance of female teachers on the Middle Border. As the century sped by, fewer and fewer men were available; one by one they had left schoolteaching for one of the nation's burgeoning professions. In that gilded age of our nation's history, schoolteaching was the country boy's most reliable stepping-stone to another career, and the history of the Midwest is filled with the names of prominent men who began teaching in country schools. There they saved a bit of money, continued their education, and went on to become editors, lawyers, politicians, college professors, physicians, and writers. [Illus. 7.2]

For women, however, the Midwest offered few job opportunities equal to that of teaching. The pay was small, to be sure, but there were other rewards. Short school terms, status, respectability, and even the feeling of accomplishment—often connected with that awesome Protestant sense of calling—were among the many reasons young women taught in the Midwest's one-room schools.

So at the crossroads of the nineteenth and twentieth centuries, it was largely an army of young women who went out to slay the dragon "ignorance" throughout the Midwest. And they

7.2. *Schoolteaching was a stepping-stone to other professions for many young midwestern men. In 1881, Gen. John J. Pershing began his career here, teaching in the one-room Prairie Mound School in District No. 1, Chariton County, Missouri. (MSHS)*

came not from afar but from the farms, villages, and small towns of the same rural heartland that they served and whose ways they understood. It was well that they did, for how else could they have stood to board in rude farmhouses, dress in cold rooms, use outdoor privies, bathe in wash-basins or tin tubs, walk a mile or so to school, endure the strong odors of their classrooms on a winter's day, light fires in the big stoves, and clean their schoolrooms—almost all of which went with the job.

Except for some of those who came from small towns, the young women who taught the three Rs in one-room schools could ride a horse, churn butter, make their own dresses, hitch up a team of horses, milk cows, and, if need be, even work in the fields. Yet you could not always tell just by looking at them that the prim young ladies pictured with their students in front of their school-houses or graduating from a teachers' institute were accustomed to doing any of these things. Dressed in white shirtwaists and dark skirts and shod in high-buttoned shoes, they were models of neatness and cleanliness who sometimes seemed as far removed from the dust and dirt of the fields as the sun from earth. [Illus. 7.3] Only when they walked to school along a dusty road or rode or drove a horse to school and unhitched it from a buggy was it obvious that they were acquainted with things rural. [Illus. 7.4]

7.4. *When she drove to school in her buggy, it became obvious that the primly dressed teacher was familiar with things rural. District No. 10, Sheffield Township, Tippecanoe County, Indiana. (TCHA)*

7.3. *In white shirtwaists and skirts, the young women attending the county institute—most of whom were from rural homes—were models of neatness and seemingly as far removed from dusty fields as the earth from the sun. Fillmore County Teachers' Institute, 1902.* (Seventeenth Biennial Report of the Nebraska State Superintendent of Public Instruction, 1901–1902 [Lincoln, 1903], p. 362)

Usually they were young; sometimes—especially in the 1880s and 1890s—they were no more than sixteen. Many were not yet twenty. It was not unusual for the teacher to be younger than some of her students, and it is often difficult to distinguish the teacher from the students in school photographs. [Illus. 7.5] Over the years, the average age of teachers increased somewhat, but most were still nubile young ladies who taught only briefly. Comparatively few ever planned to make teaching a lifetime career, and probably only a handful thought of themselves as public servants on the cutting edge of an advancing civilization. Marriage was their principal goal, and just as men used country schoolteaching as a ladder to another career, women used it as an avenue to marriage. They taught for three or four years, then married and began raising families of their own.

Of course, there were any number of women who did make teaching a career. Those who did so, however, normally left the country for urban schoolrooms, where the pay was better and the conveniences of life were available. In time, a fair number of those who remained in rural schools became county superintendents, perhaps the only office in America to which women could be elected before they had the right to vote! At least one among their number, Agnes Samuelson, even became Iowa's superintendent of public instruction. [Illus. 7.6] Yet those who did move on to

7.5. *Who is the teacher? As in many country schools, the teacher at this school in Greene County, Ohio, is so young that she is virtually indistinguishable from her older students. (OHS)*

7.6. *Long before women had the right to vote in the Middle West, female country schoolteachers were frequently elected county superintendent. Agnes Samuelson, who began her career teaching in this schoolhouse, became Iowa's state superintendent of public instruction. (SHSI, Iowa City, Agnes Samuelson Collection)*

urban schools or to administrative positions owed much to their seasoning in the one-room schools. Nowhere else in the public schools was it possible to have such a variety of experiences, challenges, and awesome responsibilities.

In retrospect, it seems incredible that the midwesterners expected so much from their country schoolteachers. Granted, people back then expected more of their teachers than we do today, but even so, many farmers wanted their teachers to be miracle workers. The general nature of their duties was spelled out in the contracts they signed. [Illus. 7.7]. But the contracts only implied all that was expected of them. The rules and regulations the farmers adopted to govern their schools give a better idea of the teachers' duties. According to these, the teacher was expected to "at all times, exercise a firm and vigilant but prudent discipline, governing as far as possible by gentle means." [Illus. 7.8]

Following such rules was a formidable task indeed. It probably was not too difficult to "forbid the use of tobacco in any form" or to send any pupil home who had "a contagious or infectious disease" or who came to school "with offensive uncleanliness of person or clothes," even though it might not have been politic to do so. But monitoring each student's language was a challenge even in those days, when everyone knew what words were profane and obscene. "Any pupil," stated the regulations, "who shall, in or around the school premises, write or other-

wise use profane or unchaste language, or who shall draw or carve any obscene picture or representation, shall be liable to suspension or expulsion according to the nature of the case" (see Illus. 7.8, rule 5 for pupils).

In short, country schoolteachers were expected to be disciplinarians of the first order, part-time nurses for the younger pupils, counselors to the older ones, and knowledgeable in the common branches of learning from the three Rs to history, geography, grammar, and advanced arithmetic. They also had to be their own janitors, record keepers, and school administrators. And in this

7.7. *Some of the teachers' duties were spelled out in the contracts they signed, which often included the grades they had made on the county teachers' examination. (Contract, Dist. No. 2, Elba Twp., Dodge Co., Wis., School Records, SHSW)*

Rules and Regulations

FOR THE GOVERNMENT OF THE SCHOOL

District No. _____   Town of _____

SUPERINTENDENT DISTRICT NO. 1,

Dane County, Wisconsin.

FOR TEACHERS.

1. The Teacher is required to be in the school room at least fifteen minutes before the time fixed for the morning session to commence, and at least five minutes before the time for the afternoon session to commence.

2. The Teacher shall maintain a personal supervision over the pupils during the time of recess, and at noon intermission, preventing any ill doing, and counselling them to engage in such sports as may be healthful and innocent.

3. Teachers will be expected to arrange their classes with reference to the course of text books adopted by the District Board, as nearly as possible, and shall not be obliged to hear recitations or form classes in any other.

4. Each Teacher is required to keep a Daily Record of the attendance of pupils, noting tardiness and conduct, to place upon the walls or black board a daily programme of recitations and study, and to make out all reports required by the County Superintendent.

5. The Teacher is required to grade the school as far as possible according to the circular published by the State Superintendent, entitled "Grading System for the Country Schools," also to follow the course of study, as far as practicable, arranged in the above mentioned circular.

6. It shall be the imperative duty of the Teacher to labor earnestly for punctuality and regular attendance on the part of the pupils.

7. The Teacher may require a reasonable excuse from parents for the absence or tardiness of pupils.

8. The Teacher shall have power to make such restrictions upon and requirements of the pupils, and establish such regulations as shall, in his or her judgment, be necessary for the good of the school, subject to the approval of the District Board.

9. Whenever, from misconduct, the good order of the school shall demand, the teacher may suspend scholars from school, reporting the same to the District Board at the close of the day; and no scholar thus suspended shall be re-admitted without consent of the District Board and the Teacher.

10. The teacher shall see that the school house is kept neat and clean and forbid the use of tobacco in any form.

11. The Teacher shall be entitled to the respect and obedience of the pupils, and shall, at all times, exercise a firm and vigilant but prudent discipline, governing as far as possible by gentle means.

FOR PUPILS.

1. Every pupil attending this school must be promptly supplied with the necessary books required. If there are parents too poor to furnish necessary books, the School Board will see that such children are provided for.

2. Pupils are expected to enter school at the beginning of the term and attend regularly and punctually, obey all directions of the teacher, observe good order, be careful in deportment, courteous and respectful to the Teacher and school mates.

3. In case of absence or tardiness a satisfactory and reasonable excuse shall be rendered to the Teacher.

4. Any pupil injuring school house, yard, fence, furniture or other school property shall make the same good in money or satisfactory repairs, and no pupil shall be allowed the privilege of the school, if he or his parents or guardian neglect to make good such damages.

5. Any pupil who shall, in or around the school premises, write or otherwise use profane or unchaste language, or who shall draw or carve any obscene picture or representation, shall be liable to suspension or expulsion according to the nature of the case.

6. No pupil shall be received or continued in school known to be afflicted with a contagious or infectious disease, or to come from a family where such disease prevails.

7. Any pupil coming to school with offensive uncleanliness of person or clothes shall be sent home to be properly prepared for school.

MISCELLANEOUS.

1. As visiting school tends to give life and animation, parents and guardians are requested to visit the school as often as possible, and District Board to visit them at least once a month.

2. The District Board are expected to act in compliance with the Amendment to Section 2, Chapter 121, Laws of 1879 and hold a special school meeting for the purpose of hearing the cause for the non-attendance of pupils upon the public schools. And it is furthermore expected that all law abiding citizens will see that the above mentioned law is fulfilled to the letter, remembering that the success of the school depends largely upon the regular attendance of pupils.

3. The wages of Teachers shall be governed by grade of their certificates, subject to modifications as to their success in former teaching. No Teacher should, seldom if ever, teach the school on a license.

4. It shall be the duty of the District Board to see that the school house is in a proper condition for school use and to make such repairs at any time as they may deem proper.

Adopted by the District Board at a regular meeting of said Board, held at _____

this _____ day of _____ 188 .

[Signed] _____

_____ Director,

_____ Treasurer,

_____ Clerk,
DISTRICT BOARD.

7.8. Rules and regulations governing country teachers were made clear in their schools' record books. (Emery School, Dist. No. 3, Albion Twp., Dane Co., Wis., School Records, SHSW)

7.9. In the early 1900s, a few country teachers were trained in model schools like this one established on the campus of Kirksville Normal School in Kirksville, Missouri. (Pickler Memorial Library, NE Mo. State Univ.)

earlier age, before modern educators determined that being a good example was not an effective way to teach values, they were expected to be virtuous models for their charges.

In return for all this, the only benefits the teachers received—aside from their pay—were the districts' promises to keep the schoolhouses in good repair and furnish the fuel. They had no sick leaves and no pensions. They had no unions, and a teachers' strike was as unthinkable as smoking on the school grounds. There was no such thing as teacher appreciation week, and although some country newspaper editors wrote kindly of them, few rhapsodized over "our dedicated teachers." True, farmers and their families generally appreciated their teachers' efforts, and they often showed it in little ways.

But inevitably there were disgruntled parents

who criticized and even spread unpleasant rumors about teachers, and the area's educators often disparaged their teaching and constantly complained of their lack of preparation—not without reason. Many young women began teaching with only a country school education and no more experience than helping to drill younger students. By the early 1900s, however, virtually all country teachers had received some formal training. A few had been trained in the normal schools established throughout the Midwest in the late 1800s. Some of these, like Kirksville Normal in Kirksville, Missouri, had gone so far as to build model one-room schools on their campuses for training prospective country teachers. [Illus. 7.9] In the early 1900s, a growing number of high schools offered courses for aspiring rural teachers. Many young farm girls enrolled in such courses once they had passed those stiff eighth-grade county examinations. [Illus. 7.10]

Before World War I, some student teachers were even being trained by observing experienced country teachers in action. In 1914, a country school near Cameron, Missouri, had been fitted with seats in the rear of the room from which future teachers might observe all that took place. [Illus. 7.11] But this technique was by no means universal. Neither high schools nor normal schools trained many country teachers

7.10. *Women who aspired to be teachers in the early 1900s and had passed the eighth-grade examination could receive additional training in the normal courses offered by high schools. Normal training class, Auburn High School, 1907.* (Twentieth Biennial Report of the State Superintendent of Public Instruction, Nebraska, 1907–1908 *[York, n.d.], opp. p. 130)*

7.11. *In 1914, a country school near Cameron, Missouri, provided an opportunity for student teachers to observe experienced teachers at work.* (Sixty-fifth Report of the Public Schools of the State of Missouri, 1915 *[Jefferson City, n.d.], opp. p. 32)*

before the First World War. For years, high schools were outside the reach of most farm children, even in the 1900s. Those who attended the normals were usually absorbed by urban schools and rarely returned to their roots in the country. The result was that well into the twentieth century, most country schoolteachers were trained in county teacher institutes.

The training provided in the institutes was better than conventional wisdom supposed. Normally lasting only a few weeks in the summer, the programs were arranged by the county superintendents, who publicized the dates and details of the events in the county newspapers. [Illus. 7.12] Such announcements generated a round of activity and a sense of anticipation among young people in rural areas, some of whom visited the county seat only once a year. In spite of the warning that the institute was not for a "mere good time," the prospective participants looked forward to having just that and made preparations to attend weeks in advance. They sent away for the official course of study they would need, made new dresses, and answered the advertisements of those offering room and board to institute teachers. [Illus. 7.13] Still, it was clear to most aspiring teachers that the institute was not just for fun and games. County superintendents never let their prospective teachers forget that the purpose of the institute was to prepare for the teachers' examinations. The county superinten-

dent in Lafayette County, Wisconsin, made the point by announcing the dates of the teachers' examinations and the dates of the institute at the same time. [Illus. 7.14]

The county teacher institutes were among the most practical and efficient teacher training programs ever devised. Gathering in the county seat's high school or sometimes at the courthouse for their classes, the students were taught everything from grammar to algebra by professional teachers who were usually from one of the nearby normal schools. And because time was limited, studies at the institutes focused more on subject matter than method; in other words, they covered what to teach rather than how to teach it. Not until institute instructors became more professionally oriented did courses in teaching method begin to creep into the county institute curriculum.

In the dreaded examinations that came at the end of the institutes, students were questioned on all the common branches of learning, a bit on

7.12. *County teacher institutes lasting for a few weeks in the summer were the midwestern country teachers' principal source of training. Arranged by the county superintendent, they were publicized in the county newspapers. (Eldorado Educational Advance, May 1, 1894, p. 1)*

NORMAL INSTITUTE.
1894.

The Normal Institute will soon be here. Scores of our young people are getting ready to attend. Every person who expects to be with us should remember that—

"He most lives, who thinks most,
Feels the noblest, acts the best."

And that while our Normal Institute is, and will be a great social gathering, it is not for that purpose alone, that we come to the county seat to attend it. We come to gather inspiration, to help our oft discouraged souls to keep in view the lofty ideal always high above the true teacher, and to strive for means of obtaining the glorious heights where true knowledge dwells in her purity and sublimity.

So we hope our young friends will guard against preparing for a mere good time. Institute work should mean hard work, study and close application—and every one should be ready to devote himself or herself to these objects, otherwise the aim of the Institute is defeated. The social features follow of themselves, and are better enjoyed after duty well done.

7.13. *Young people intending to enroll in the county teacher institute sent for the course of study advertised in the county weekly. (MSHS)*

TO TEACHERS !

The official course of study for Teachers' Institutes has been completely revised by Hon. John R. Kirk, State Superintendent of schools and a corps of able assistants. . . . .

EVERY LINE IN THE WORK IS

NEW AND UP-TO-DATE,

and no live teacher can afford be without a copy. It is larger than any previous edition, printed from clear, new type, on good paper, and will be sent to any address for **10 cents** for the paper binding and **50c** for the muslin binding. Those ordering the paper edition should send one cent for postage and the muslin edition two cents. When 100 copies or more are ordered, express charges will be pre-paid.

Ready June 5, 1895.

Orders should be accompanied by the cash and will be filled in the order of reception.

ADDRESS

JOURNAL-DEMOCRAT,
WARRENSBURG, MO.

pedagogy, and, in the early 1900s, even on agriculture. The tests were not objective, and they were not easy, which explains why so much time had to be spent on subject matter. Not everyone succeeded in spite of the drills. Some fell by the wayside before the institutes ended, and others failed the examinations. Of the 282 students who attended the 1894 institute in Eldorado, Kansas, 196 took the examination, but only 121 passed.

FALL EXAMINATIONS.

DARLINGTON, Wis., July 20, 1882. The La Fayette County Teachers' Institute will be held at Darlington, commencing August 21st, and continue two weeks. Profs. H. C. NYE, of Platteville and H. JANE, of Shullsburg, will conduct the institute.

I shall be ready to assist teachers to secure board.

I shall expect all the teachers that are not teaching to attend the institute. The examinations for the fall of 1882 will be held as follows:

Darlington—During the institute.
Gratiot—Monday and Tuesday, September 4 and 5.
Belmont—Wednesday and Thursday, Sept. 6 and 7.
Shullsburg—Monday and Tuesday, September 11 and 12.
Argyle—Friday and Saturday, September 15 and 16.

Examinations will commence the first day at 10 o'clock. No applicants admitted after the first day. Applicants will come prepared with pens, ink and legal cap paper. No private examinations will be given except for sickness or absence from the State.

Those interested in education are invited to attend both institute and examinations.
C. G. THOMAS,
County Supt.

7.14. *The teachers' examinations, which were given at the end of the institute, hung like a gray cloud over those who attended. (Lafayette Co., Wis., Democrat, Aug. 25, 1882, p. 1)*

Of those who passed, 66 did so with a third-grade certificate, the lowest of all certificates.

For those who succeeded, it was a glorious day when they received their teaching certificates. Their names appeared in the county papers, and friends and neighbors offered congratulations. All they needed were schools to teach in. Sometimes school directors from the county's one-room schools came to the institutes, sought out those who already had certificates, and employed them on the spot. But it was not uncommon for a newly certified teacher to win a position through the influence of a friend or relative. Indeed, she might even be invited to teach in the very school she had attended. Often the county superintendent, who knew of every vacancy in the county, suggested where new teachers might apply. This could be done by writing a letter, which might or might not give an inkling of a teacher's qualifications. [Illus. 7.15] Usually, however, teachers drove their buggies into the countryside to meet with members of school boards whose schools had no teacher. More than one interview took place in the fields where the board members were hard at work.

Once a teacher was promised the position, the next step was to find a place in the district to live and to prepare for the first day of school. It's virtually impossible to appreciate what it must have been like to be a young, inexperienced country

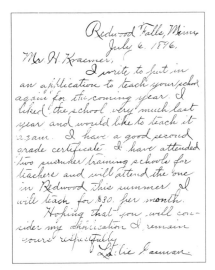

7.16. *Welch's Teachers' Classification Register told the country teacher all she needed to know about how to organize her school. (Emery School, Dist. No. 3, Albion Twp., Dane Co., Wis., School Records, SHSW)*

7.15. To secure teaching positions, some teachers interviewed with school board members at the institute, some visited the members on their farms, and some wrote letters of application, which might or might not suggest their qualifications. (Minn. Historical Archives, St. Paul)

schoolteacher on the first day of school. If she had not come from a distinctly farm background, it could be unnerving indeed. She rose early in the sometimes embarrassingly close quarters of the home where she boarded, dressed with some difficulty, visited the outdoor privy, washed herself in a tin basin, breakfasted with the family, and walked perhaps a mile or more to school. The schoolhouse in which she taught was often isolated, possibly no nearer than a mile to the closest home. It might or might not have a well; it might have two privies, one, or none at all. If the school was dirty, she had to clean it; if it was a cold morning, she had to build a fire in the stove. Before her were some fifteen to twenty-five children ranging in age from five to sixteen or seventeen, and she faced the daunting task of organizing them into a school.

Fortunately, she had help. She might have been taught a bit about school organization at the institute, but if not, she was still not entirely lost. At her school she had Welch's *Teachers' Classification Register*, or one like it, to tell her everything she needed to know about how to organize her school. [Illus. 7.16] Those who have wondered how country teachers managed to teach so much to so many children of different

ages all in one room need only examine this ingenious compilation—one of the most widely used books of records and instructions in the Midwest. The *Classification Register* could be arranged to fit any state's course of study, even when country schools became graded like urban schools.

Before their division into eight grades, country schools were classified, and the *Register* showed the teacher how to classify her school into the primary, middle, and upper forms, or sometimes into primary, intermediate, and grammar grades. It listed the branches of learning that should be given to each grade group and even gave instructions on how to present each branch. In teaching language to the primary B class, for example, the teacher was instructed to lead the pupils to talk in complete sentences; in writing, they were to learn how to use capitals and the rules for terminal punctuation marks. [Illus. 7.17]

Included in the *Register* were suggestions on arranging a daily schedule. Mina O'Connor's "Daily Programme of Recitation and Study" for her school in District No. 3, Dane County, Wisconsin, shows how she managed her time, following the *Register's* instructions. The material under "Recitations" confirms that her entire day was spent in recitations, which might lead one to speculate that recesses and the noontime break were originated more for the sake of the country schoolteacher than for the children. [Illus. 7.18] Of the twenty-five recitations Mina O'Connor held each day, nine were devoted to reading, and with good reason.

Record of ... ... STUDY FOR COMMON SCHOOLS.

PRIMARY GRADE. B. CLASS.

Reading.—Charts and First Reader. Pupils should be able to recognize at sight about fifty familiar words before taking up First Reader. Teach script and printed forms from chart or blackboard, associating each form—"Word Picture"—with the thing itself, or picture of it, or with some expression of the thought represented. Keep a list of all words learned, upon the blackboard, and add new words as soon as learned. Gradually call attention to the letters which compose each word.

Writing. With long pencils on slate (*See Speer's Manual, pages 13 and 16.*)

Language.—In connection with all work, reading especially, lead pupils to talk in complete sentences; correct common errors of speech. In writing, teach then the simple rules for capitals in proper names, in beginning sentences, and the word I, and rules for use of terminal marks (question mark (?) period (.) &c.) (See Manual, pages 12 and 13.)

Spelling.—Taught in connection with other lessons. (See Manual, page 11.)

Numbers.—Counting and adding objects, as pegs, beans, balls on the numeral frame, etc. All possible combinations of numbers, the result not to exceed 10. For some time objects should be associated with figures, to give the idea of numbers; teach the grouping of numbers by using pegs, beans, grains of corn, etc.; likewise by actual measurement of feet in a yard, dimes in a dollar, etc. Adding simple columns of not more than ten figures, the result not to exceed thirty. Counting by one's to one hundred, by two's to fifty. Numbers of two and three figures read at sight, and written on slates. Roman notation to L. (See Manual, page 12.)

General Lessons.—ETHICS—Conversational, on order, etiquette, cleanliness, etc.

GENERAL—Talks on the human body, animals, etc.

OBJECT LESSONS—The square, oblong, ball, etc. Draw on slates or paper.

COLOR LESSONS.—Common colors, as red, yellow, blue, green, orange, purple, etc., to be distinguished. (See Manual, page 9.)

Busy Work.—Embracing much of the foregoing work in numbers, reading, etc., to be done on slates. Keep children employed. Vary the work.

A CLASS.

Reading.—Second Reader. Teach long and short vowels with their diacritical marks. (For further suggestions see Manual, pages 11 and 14.)

Writing.—(See suggestions in Manual, pages 13 and 16.)

Spelling.—Words of reading lesson for following recitation, spelled phonetically and by letter, and the pronunciation repeated until pupils can pronounce all new words fluently; then at seats pupils write each new word in two or more sentences, showing its various use. (For further suggestions see Manual pages 15 and 16.)

Language.—Work continued in B Class. (See Manual, pages 12, 13 and 15.)

Numbers.—Drill in rapid combinations of all the digits, adding single and double columns. Subtraction of simple numbers, multiplication with one figure in the multiplier. Reading and writing numbers to six places. Roman numbers to C. Multiplication table completed. (See Manual, pages 12 and 14.)

General Lessons.—Continue as in B Class.

Busy Work, Continued.—The teacher can easily devise new, varied, and profitable employment for seat work—such as number work, writing words of reading lesson in sentences formed by the pupil, drawing, writing, etc.

Physical Training.—Pupils will grow tired and dull. A new supply of fresh air and a two-minute exercise in calisthenics will invigorate pupils for renewed effort and often preclude mischief.

INTERMEDIATE GRADE. B. CLASS.

Reading.—Third Reader. Correct faulty enunciation. Make pupils familiar with new and difficult words. Train them to see and grasp sentences or elements of sentences quickly and thus express the idea naturally. The painful effort of pupils to group words in reading, comes from trying to pronounce unfamiliar words which should have been previously learned, and often begets "drawling." Train the pupils to express the thoughts of the author in language entirely their own. Read selections requiring great care in articulation. In this class the pupils should own and use a Dictionary. (See Manual, pages 16, 17 and 18.)

Writing.—Daily Drills in writing should be given to every class of Intermediate and Grammar Grades.—(See suggestions in Manual, pages 13 and 16.)

Spelling.—About one-third of the Complete Spelling Book; also all difficult words of other lessons. No word should be merely spelled, and passed over without the assurance that the pupil can pronounce it fluently, and use it in various sentences correctly.

Language Work.—Continued in connection with reading lesson. Compose sentences using all the new words. Pupils write up the substance of the reading lesson in language entirely their own. Cause children to talk about the reading lesson, pictures, flowers—anything, and lead them to express their thoughts in well rounded sentences.

LETTER WRITING should be made a prominent feature of the work of this class.

Thus far the language work is outlined in connection with reading, but its importance should not be overlooked on that account. (See Manual, page 21.)

Arithmetic.—Elementary Arithmetic through Division. Teachers should insist upon a clear, concise analysis of each problem. Continue Drills to secure accuracy and rapidity.

Geography.—Location and direction of objects in familiar places, as schoolyard, neighborhood, township, county and state. Globe lessons—the earth as a whole as to form, size, land and water forms; motions of the earth causing day and night. (See Manual, page 20)

Physiology.—Oral lessons daily. (See Manual, pages 22, 23a and 23b.)

General Lessons—Continue as in last Grade. Elementary Science, conversational lessons on History, Animals, Plants, etc. Tell pupils about the various occupations, industries and materials used, and excite interest, thought and investigation. Remember that the professional teacher stimulates the pupil's mind to a desire for knowledge before giving it.

A CLASS.

Reading.—Fourth Reader. Attention to the rules and principles of good reading. Cultivate the habit of reading "to get the thought" clearly; cultivate the habit of attentive listening by having one pupil read while the rest listen; call on some pupil to state clearly what was read; call attention to the ability of different pupils to bring out the thought of the author clearly. Continue use of Dictionary as in third grade. Analyze words; prefixes and suffixes; word grouping in sentences—oral and written. (See Manual, page 18)

Spelling.—About second third of book; also continue spelling the difficult words of other lessons.

Language.—Continue work of B Class. Parts of speech and their uses, their subdivisions and properties. Pupils may use a text book on this, as the teacher thinks best. Every point should be mastered in oral or written work, and each should be thoroughly mastered before another is taken up. (See Manual, page 22.)

Arithmetic.—Factoring and its applications; Fractions, common and decimal, and compound numbers. (See Manual, pages 19 and 20.)

Geography.—Elementary Geography completed. Pupils should have drawn maps of Europe, Asia and Africa, and taken a general survey of each; topical outline of your own State.

Physiology.—Oral lessons in physiology with the B Class.

General Lessons.—Lessons on the human body and health lessons continued. Continue elementary lessons in Civil Government and History. Astronomy and Natural Philosophy; at least give occasional lessons on government of the school District, Township, County, State and Nation in outline.

Inculcate in pupils patriotism, regard for rights of individuals, and obedience to laws, in connection with lessons in practical morality.

GRAMMAR GRADE. B CLASS.

Reading.—Fifth Reader completed. In this grade it would be well to introduce some such supplementary books as Hawthorne's "Easy Chair Series" of Historical Readers, or their equivalent, in connection with the Fifth Reader. These books will give a great variety of work.

Writing.—Continued as in former Grades. (See Manual, page 31.)

Spelling.—Complete and review the Spelling Book.

Grammar.—The Complete English Grammar, about first half of book; analysis, parsing, syntactical criticisms, and corrections; composition to apply principles of Grammar. (See Manual, page 28.)

Arithmetic.—Review common fractions thoroughly for accuracy and rapidity; also decimal fractions; master the tables of weights and measures; begin percentage. (See Manual, page 27.)

7.17. *Instructions for classifying country schools and teaching each subject were found on the inside covers of Welch's* Teachers' Classification Register. *(Ise School, Dist. No. 37, Osborne Co., Kans., School Records, KSHS)*

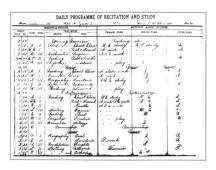

7.18. *Mina O'Connor's "Daily Programme of Recitation and Study" for the year 1895–96 included twenty-five recitations during the day. (Emery School, Dist. No. 3, Albion Twp., Dane Co., Wis., School Records, SHSW)*

become, but it was no small task even then. Some of the school's finances depended on this chore, so the numbers of students in school, their tardiness, and their absences all had to be noted in the daily records and given to the clerk of the school board, who gave them to the county superintendent. There were also places for student grades to be recorded, which was a major advance over previous practice. Surprisingly, it was apparently not until about 1884, the copyright date on Welch's first *Register*, that a system of grading country schoolchildren was developed.

For years, children in the one-room schools had no course of study and no real classification.

In midwestern country schools no subject was as important as reading. Day in and day out, the younger students trooped to her desk for their reading lessons; the older ones, books in hand, lined up before her to read one after the other, with all the school witnessing how well or how poorly they did. For some it was exhilarating, for others excruciating, but there was no way out. They had to learn to read. [Illus. 7.19]

Classification registers also contained detailed instructions on keeping various kinds of records. Record keeping was not the awful burden it has

7.19. *Like these students from Subdistrict No. 7 in Oneida Township, Delaware County, Iowa, the older children lined up to read aloud before their classmates and the teacher almost every day. (SHSI, Iowa City, Huftalen Collection)*

They simply read through the readers until they completed the sixth; then they were through. No records of their progress were kept, and time and again, when they returned to school after missing a term or two, they began all over again, which led to the old midwestern adage that "no one ever finishes a country school." But the development of a course of study, followed by schools throughout an entire state, gave students a standard set of subjects to be mastered, and Welch's *Register* provided a system for marking their progress. On one side of the record book the teacher listed the names and numbers of students and the grades they had made in each of the subjects. On the other, she noted each student's form—primary, middle, or upper—and class—A, B, or C. On this page the teacher identified each student by the number preceding his or her name on the opposite page and commented briefly on the status of particular students. Here she also remarked on the textbooks used, the pages covered, the status of each class, and where each class should begin the next term. [Illus. 7.20]

Some indication of the level of work required of country children in the one-room schools before World War I can be inferred from the notes left by Cecelia Graves relating to the upper

7.21. *An indication of the level of work required by children in the Midwest's one-room schools can be seen in this teacher's record of students in the upper and middle forms in the Emery School, District No. 3, Albion Township, Dane County, Wisconsin. (School Records, SHSW)*

7.20. *Teachers followed a course of study that had been developed for one-room schools in the Midwest. They recorded students' grades and left remarks regarding the students' progress for their successors. (Dist. No. 37, Osborne Co., Kans., School Records, KSHS)*

and middle forms of her Wisconsin school in 1912. [Illus. 7.21] These remarks were intended for the succeeding teacher. This practice was especially important, since even into the twentieth century, teachers normally taught no more than one term in the same school. Apparently, no one knows exactly why. Rural people probably felt that it was better not to permit a teacher to become too well entrenched in the community and school, lest she build up harmful alliances that might jeopardize the community's peace. Whatever the reason, this was the custom, and after each school term, the county weeklies were filled with announcements of teachers closing out "one successful school" and securing another for the next term.

The school term usually closed with a program, which was only one of several programs the teachers were expected to produce during a school term. Thanksgiving and Christmas, Arbor Day, plus Lincoln's and Washington's birthdays were all celebrated in the country schools. For these special events, parents flocked to the little schoolhouses to see their children perform, and the quality of these programs was one standard by which rural people measured the success of their teachers. It was their way of knowing whether the teachers had really taught their children anything at all.

Because of the nature of the one-room school, the last day of the term was nearly always filled with touching farewells, as students and their families parted with the teacher. So that they might be remembered by their students, some teachers gave their students souvenir cards containing their pictures and the names of all the pupils in the school. [Illus. 7.22] Other teachers presented their students with cards expressing those bittersweet sentiments so familiar to rural Americans generations ago. "My Dear Pupil" in Illus. 7.23 was much like today's standard greeting-card verse, but no matter. Doubtless it expressed the teacher's true feelings about her students, whom she had come to know so much more intimately than urban teachers could know theirs.

A special relationship between country teachers and their students was frequently forged, even though they taught in each school for only one term. Their schools were so small that they knew the names of all their pupils by the end of the first day. And because their students came from only a few families, the teachers knew the parents almost as well as they knew the children. This was almost inevitable because of the parents' interest and involvement in what was peculiarly "their school." According to the souvenir for

7.23. *Sentimental cards were among country teachers' favorite parting gifts to their students. (Walter M. Anderson Collection, Emporia, Kans.)*

Prairie School in District No. 166, Sedgwick County, Kansas, in 1902–03 there were five Frey children, three Gables, four Peatses, two McKennas, four Vulgamores, and four Ramsdales. Under the circumstances, it was inevitable that Rose Budd, their teacher, would know her students and their families almost as well as if she had taught in the school for two years instead of three months. [Illus. 7.24]

Although the teachers' incessant switching of schools was obviously not the best system ever devised, it did have certain advantages. Natu-

7.22. *The last day of the school term was filled with touching farewells. Some teachers gave students mementos displaying their pictures and the names of their students. (Walter M. Anderson Collection, Emporia, Kans.)*

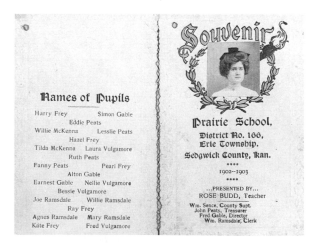

7.24. *Country teachers formed special and long-lasting bonds with their students and their families. In the Prairie School in Sedgwick County, Kansas, no student was without another member of his or her family in attendance. (KSHS)*

7.25. Until well into the twentieth century, it was unusual for a midwestern country teacher to teach more than a single term in one school, but there were exceptions. The same teacher taught here at the Rosary School in District No. 11, St. Louis County, Missouri, for twenty-four years. (Sixty-second Report of the Public Schools of the State of Missouri, 1911 [Jefferson City, n.d.], opp. p. 32)

rally, it did not permit students to benefit from their good teachers for very long, but the reverse was also true. Furthermore, the move to new schools and strange surroundings may have made teachers more conscientious and less prone to the familiarity that might lead to carelessness. Finally, the system made it less likely that teachers would become overly friendly with students or have favorites.

Nevertheless, the great teacher turnover after every school term was abhorrent to all developing pedagogical theories. Educational experts worked night and day to change the practice, and by the early 1900s they had succeeded here and there. The little Rosary School in District No. 11, St. Louis County, Missouri, which had fifty-four students in 1911, had retained the same teacher for twenty-four years by that time. [Illus. 7.25] All the Missouri teachers shown in Illus. 7.26 made the teaching honor roll in 1910 by teaching more than five consecutive terms in the same rural schools. One of them, Louis C. Saeger, had taught in District No. 35 of St. Charles County since 1877—the longest continuous service in a rural school in the state at the time. These were the exceptions, however. The vast majority drifted out of teaching long before they either received professional training or burned out.

7.26. The trend of country teachers staying in the same school for longer periods began sometime before World War I. Those pictured here were honored for having taught more than five consecutive terms at the same country schools. (Sixty-second Report of the Public Schools of the State of Missouri, 1911 [Jefferson City, n.d.], opp. p. 67)

Few found teaching easy. They had to board in often unsuitable homes; they were bound by their contracts and the nature of things to sweep floors, build fires, teach all subjects to various-aged children, and hold as many as thirty recitations a day—all for a mere $30 or $40 a month! But those who taught in the one-room schools remembered the pleasures as well as the pain. They recalled oyster suppers, debates, spelling bees, and socials at the schoolhouse; friendly people; and a job that gave meaning to their lives. Quite a few of them found their husbands in the districts where they taught and eventually used their experiences and education to help their own children.

7.27. Numerous prominent men were taught in midwestern one-room schools by teachers who never realized the contribution they were making to the region and the nation. Dale Carnegie went to this school—the Rose Hill School in Nodaway County, Missouri. (MSHS)

Though yesterday's one-room schoolteachers could scarcely have been aware of the magnitude of their contributions to midwestern culture, it is clear in retrospect that they were immense. Over the years they taught generations of young people to read, write, and figure. They instilled in them the moral values of Western civilization and a love of country. They gave their students a smattering of the world's best literature and started more than a few of them on the road to the area's great colleges and universities, from which they emerged to become the professionals of the late nineteenth and early twentieth centuries. [Illus. 7.27]

Yet in that age of rising cities, booming industry, rapid change, and apparent progress, both country schoolteachers and one-room schoolhouses seemed woefully out of step with the rest of society. To the growing number of professional educators who were rapidly establishing the Midwest's educational bureaucracy, one-room schools were poor schools and the area's number-one educational problem.

Chapter
8

Poor, Poor,
Country Schools

8.1. *Streetcar lines, opera houses, telephone lines, and gas lamps lined the main streets of even modest midwestern towns in the 1880s and 1890s. They revolutionized urban living and reflected the cultural aspirations of small-town citizens. Main Street, Fort Scott, Kansas. (KSHS)*

Ask the average urban American what he knows about one-room schools and he is likely to say that they were pioneer schools, designed to meet frontier conditions and abandoned when those conditions ended. This is but one of the many misconceptions Americans have about midwestern country schools. True, they began as pioneer schools, but thousands remained in operation for decades after frontier conditions had disappeared. Long before the superintendent of the census startled Americans in 1890 with the announcement that the nation no longer had a frontier line, most of the area's one-roomers had ceased to be pioneer schools. By 1900, the old log and sod schoolhouses reminiscent of pioneer days were gone or fading fast.

From Kansas and Nebraska east to Ohio, and from Missouri north to Minnesota and the Dakotas, the farmers had built their second and sometimes their third country schools and greatly improved them. They had equipped them with patented seats, libraries, maps, globes, and, in some places, organs. They had beautified the school grounds, built fences for the school yards, dug wells, installed pumps, and made personal sacrifices for their children's education that were out of all proportion to those made by urbanites. Yet the notion that one-room schoolhouses were primitive, pioneer schools lingered on.

The region's educators regarded them with contempt. Year after year, their reports lamenting the country schools' poor teachers, rickety schoolhouses, inadequate playgrounds, sparse apparatus, and filthy toilets filled the area's educational reports and spilled over into the bulletins of the nation's Bureau of Education. Small schools, they said, were too small to be good. But that wasn't all. Expert opinion held that the farmers who ran them prevented progress. In the eyes of the experts, they were tightfisted and sometimes illiterate people who knew nothing about education and cared even less. "The only way I see to better the condition of the country schools," said a Michigan educator in 1879, "is to take just as much of the control out of the hands of the people as possible."

That seemed the reasonable thing to do. From the 1880s on into the twentieth century, few knowledgeable observers quibbled with the criticisms that the experts heaped on one-room schools. And in fact, there was much to criticize. Hundreds of the little schools did have poor teachers; many had ramshackle schoolhouses. Some had almost no educational apparatus, and others were governed by stingy farmers who would rather build a new barn than repair a schoolhouse. Nor was it easy to argue with the professionals. More than a few of them had attended one-room schools themselves and knew firsthand of the conditions. Some had even begun their teaching careers in them and loved to tell humorously condescending stories of their experiences among the farmers. But their disdain for country schools was not solely a product of their experiences and the obvious flaws of rural education; it was magnified by the contrast they saw between conditions in the countryside and those in the area's burgeoning towns and cities in the last quarter of the nineteenth century.

The nation's townspeople had always had a certain degree of contempt for those from the country, but it was never more marked in the Middle West than in the Gilded Age, when Jefferson's noble farmers became hicks and even villagers ridiculed their overalls and tanned faces

8.2. At century's end, midwestern country roads were unpaved and often ungraded. Winding their way through hills and valleys, they isolated farm people in winter and spring. This road is near the Deckard School in Brown County, Indiana. (Ind. Univ. Foundation)

when they came to town on Saturday afternoons. This deepening disdain for farms and farmers was largely due to the era's many innovations in urban development, which made the differences between town and country living more noticeable than ever before. Indoor plumbing, gas, electricity, and central heating had become commonplace in urban homes by the 1890s, and new modes of transportation changed the faces of towns and cities. Cities expanded and suburbs developed as newly paved streets and new streetcar lines took people to rural homes on the cities' fringes—where, somewhat ironically, they wished to live—and back to the cities—where they wished to work. By the mid-1880s, there was free mail delivery to homes in towns as small as 10,000 inhabitants; that plus the expansion of telephone lines brought the world to urban doors. At the same time, new museums, opera houses, and Carnegie libraries—monuments to the cultural aspirations of middle-class midwesterners—flourished on the main streets of even the most modest midwestern towns. [Illus. 8.1]

But in the countryside, time seemed to have stood still. At the century's end, the pattern of life there had changed little since the Civil War. Children growing up in the rural Midwest still lived in a world of plowed fields, wooded hills, and

8.3. *Country children grew up in homes without modern conveniences, endured the heat and cold of upstairs rooms, rose early to do their outdoor chores, and frequently slushed their way to school over muddy roads. (Mich. Historical Collections, Bentley Historical Library, Univ. of Mich.)*

8.4. *In midwestern towns and cities, large imposing schoolhouses—equipped with the latest school apparatus and the finest facilities—stood in sharp contrast to the area's one-room schools. Harrison School, Topeka, Kansas. (KSHS)*

open plains stretching, like their imaginations, far beyond the horizon. It was a place of distances in which no gathering place—neither school nor church nor store nor post office—was close at hand. To be sure, country roads wound their way through hills and valleys to end up, finally, in a country town or village. But these roads were unimproved and scarcely passable during some seasons of the year. For many country children, the world they knew barely reached beyond the county seat, where their fathers paid their taxes and where they visited only occasionally. [Illus. 8.2]

Compared with the lives of middle-class urban children, those of country children were hard and lonely. Living in homes that had no central heat, no indoor plumbing, and no electricity, they dressed and undressed in cold upstairs rooms in winter, bathed—when they bathed—in tubs placed beside the kitchen stove, went outdoors to use the toilet, and studied at the kitchen table by the light of a kerosene lamp. They rose early in the morning and spent an hour or more in the barn or chicken house doing chores. [Illus. 8.3] Then they walked a mile or more to the country schoolhouse, where their system of education, in the view of educators, had fallen far behind that in the cities.

The revolutionary changes that made life easier in the cities and towns in the 1880s and 1890s had been accompanied by changes in education.

New schoolhouses—large, imposing buildings taking up half a block or more—had the finest school apparatus available. Their playgrounds were beautified and filled with up-to-date recreational equipment. Many even had gymnasiums for supervised games and exercises. [Illus. 8.4] The new schools had up-to-date libraries, but urban children also had access to public libraries and museums to enrich their education. Some city school systems even had their own museums. For example, the educational museum in St. Louis in the early 1900s not only had rooms for viewing its many materials but also had a van to cart the materials around to schools within the city. [Illus. 8.5]

These important advantages were accompanied by a relatively new system devised to educate the growing hordes of urban children. By the time the old century faded from view, the professionals had already seized control of the urban schools, developed an educational bureaucracy, and created up-to-date graded schools that were as efficient as the new businesses to which they were often compared. We are so accustomed to how our schools are organized that we give no thought to our children being grouped in classes according to their ages and passed from grade to

8.5. *New urban schools had fine libraries. The St. Louis school system had an educational museum with a van to deliver educational materials to the city's schools. (U.S. Bureau of Education, Bulletin no. 48 [Washington, D.C.: GPO, 1915], p. 13)*

8.6. *In urban schoolhouses, each teacher had her own well-appointed classroom, such as this one at the Farley School in Richmond, Indiana. (Twentieth Biennial Report of the State Superintendent of Public Instruction, Indiana, 1899–1900 [Indianapolis, 1901], p. 670)*

grade until they finish school. But there was a time before the Civil War when urban children of all ages were herded into one big auditorium for study and shunted from there to small rooms to recite their lessons to other students who were not much older than themselves. The system was clumsy and fraught with disciplinary problems. In the St. Louis schools, where it prevailed in 1858, as many as a hundred incidents of corporal punishment occurred each day in a school of fewer than five hundred students, as schoolmasters struggled to maintain order in the big auditoriums.

Oddly enough, it was a new kind of school building designed by Massachusetts educator John Philbrick that helped change all that. His new building had twelve separate rooms of about equal size, one for each class (or possibly two classes) of children of approximately the same age. Each room had its own teacher and school apparatus. [Illus. 8.6] In this orderly classroom of perhaps thirty or thirty-five students, teachers taught only one grade (certainly no more than two) the uniform lessons mandated by the principal or superintendent and held only a few recitations during the day. [Illus. 8.7] At the end of the school year, the entire class was usually passed along to the next grade in lockstep fashion—so smoothly that it seemed almost miraculous compared to what had been.

Thus a different kind of schoolhouse helped

create a new urban educational system that could educate thousands of children as efficiently as new machines could make shoes. This was the progress of which the area's educators were so proud, and it was one of the reasons that they found the one-room schools so unsatisfactory. There, sitting beside dirt roads, the little schoolhouses were so small by comparison with urban schools and so seemingly disorderly that it was little wonder educators thought them hopeless.

The small schoolhouse never seemed to be

8.7. *In urban classrooms, each teacher taught one grade—or sometimes two—of children who were approximately the same age. (Twentieth Biennial Report of the State Superintendent of Public Instruction, Indiana, 1899–1900 [Indianapolis, 1901], p. 687)*

8.8. In this photograph of the sixth grade at the Harrison School in Topeka, Kansas, nicely dressed children appear self-assured and confident. (KSHS)

quiet. All day long children aged five to sixteen marched through the one room, tramping to and from the water pail, the blackboards, the outdoor privy, and the teacher's desk, where they recited their lessons. Not infrequently, this occurred in the most forlorn of buildings. One rural inspector, visiting schools with the county superintendent in Nebraska in the early 1900s, stopped at a schoolhouse so desolate that they could look through the roof to the sky and see out the door without opening it. Some of the school's window panes were broken, and there were holes in the floor, which was separated from the earth only by thin boards. In that school was a young boy named Dick. He dragged one

8.9. Children of all ages filled the one-room Owaso School in Iowa. Their appearance—with homemade dresses, overalls out at the knees, and lack of shoes— reflects their humble surroundings and apparent lack of opportunity. (SHSI, Iowa City)

foot along the floor as he walked so that the loose sole of the old shoe he wore would not flap. Dick was only one of many in similar circumstances.

Differences in the standards of living of middle-class urban and country schoolchildren, as well as their systems of education, show up in old photographs. Illus. 8.8 and 8.9, both taken in the same era, highlight the differences that educators saw between urban and rural schools. In the first, the sixth graders at the Harrison School in Topeka, Kansas—all about the same age—are wearing well-tailored suits and dresses. Self-assured and confident, they stand proudly with their teacher. What a different story the photograph of the little Iowa school in Illus. 8.9 tells! There, children of all ages pose in front of their small schoolhouse. Dressed in homemade calico dresses and in britches and overalls out at the knees, shod in cheap high-top shoes or none at all, they look out on a world that has seemingly given them an unfair start in life. Accustomed to hard work and primitive living conditions, unused to luxuries, isolated from much of the world, and dependent on the poor, much-maligned one-room school for their education, they appear to be among the most disadvantaged children in the nation. Today they would be called underprivileged, and indeed, when the new century began, numerous observers thought of them in just that way.

Strangely, much more was being accomplished in those one-room schoolhouses than seemed possible from all outward appearances. Even in that poor Nebraska school that the rural inspector and county superintendent had visited, it was obvious that real learning was taking place. Fourteen children were hard at work there as the two officials entered the room. "Every pupil kept at his work," the inspector said. "Classes were called and dismissed in good order." And in the day's spell-down, Dick, the boy with the floppy shoe, held his place at the head of the spelling line, winning the head mark for the day.

Midwestern educators rarely commented on the real learning taking place in their region's one-room schoolhouses. Nor did they appear to pay much attention to the statistics that the U.S. commissioner of education was gathering on the

Table 8.1. Divisional Comparison of Various School Statistics, 1900

Division	Number of Teachers	Number of School Buildings	Percentage Total Population Enrolled in Schools	Percentage of Population Aged 5–18 Enrolled	Average Daily Attendance of Enrollees (%)
North Atlantic	103,732	42,433	17.32	68.09	72.43
South Atlantic	48,008	35,854	20.91	61.37	61.02
South Central	62,368	50,517	21.46	61.90	66.80
North Central	181,916	105,118	22.16	75.68	69.84
Western	24,264	13,399	19.70	81.13	69.08

SOURCE: *Report of the Commissioner of Education, 1900* (Washington, D.C.: GPO, 1901), pp. lxxii, lxxiii, lxvii, lxxvi, and lxviii.

Table 8.2. Divisional Comparison of School Revenue Derived from State and Local Taxes

Division	School Revenues Derived from State and Local Taxes		Average Amount of School Revenue per Taxpayer from Local Taxes
	% State	% Local	
North Atlantic	13.9	69.7	$9.99
South Atlantic	35.1	51.0	2.80
South Central	39.3	42.5	2.00
North Central	8.9	77.1	9.00
Western	28.2	60.5	6.85

SOURCE: *Report of the Commissioner of Education, 1900* (Washington, D.C.: GPO, 1901), p. lxxvi.

Table 8.3. School Attendance and Per-Pupil Expenditure, 1900

Division	Average Number of School Days	Average Number of Days Attended by Each Pupil Enrolled	Average Yearly Expenditure per Pupil
North Atlantic	177.1	128.3	$31.72
South Atlantic	112.0	68.3	10.68
South Central	99.7	66.6	7.34
North Central	155.6	108.7	20.85
Western	145.7	99.2	30.44

SOURCE: *Report of the Commissioner of Education, 1900* (Washington, D.C.: GPO, 1901), pp. lxix and lxxix.

nation to do so, could give their children a good elementary education.

At the beginning of the new century, the twelve midwestern states composing the North Central Division had more one-room schools and more teachers than any other section of the nation. They also led the nation in the percentage of total population enrolled in schools and were just behind the Western Division in the percentage of school-age children enrolled. Moreover, only the North Atlantic Division, comprising New England and the Middle Atlantic states and already heavily urbanized, surpassed the Midwest in the average number of pupils actually present each day. [Table 8.1] The commissioner's statistics in 1900 also showed that midwesterners, wedded to the doctrine of self-help, relied far less on state taxes and more on local taxes for their school revenues than did all other sections. Not only that, but the Midwest was second only to the North Atlantic Division in the average amount of school money raised per taxpayer. [Table 8.2] When we remember that throughout most of the period the farmers of the Midwest had few entities other than themselves to tax for the operation of their schools, these statistics are impressive evidence of the midwesterners' interest in their children's education.

Two more sets of the commissioner's statistics for 1900 are instructive. The first showed the Midwest leading all sections except the urbanized North Atlantic Division in the average number of school days and the average number of days attended by each pupil enrolled. But the second—the most negative of the North Central Division's statistics—placed the area third in the

status of education around the nation. Perhaps it simply went against reason to suppose that such poor, chaotic schools could educate anyone very well—no matter what the commissioner reported. In retrospect, the statistics offer considerable proof that parents, freed from bureaucratic restraints and with little more than the determi-

average amount it spent per pupil per year. [Table 8.3]

All these figures were less important than results, however. What did the children learn? The answer is that, at the very least, they learned to read and write. In the absence of standardized testing in the nineteenth century, we have only the census statistics on literacy to indicate how well the schools were doing. And no matter how controversial recent scholars have found them to be, they obviously give some indication of what was happening in the schools. It was surely more than coincidental that as the number of midwestern one-room schools soared, the area's illiteracy rate declined. By 1890, the people of the Midwest (North Central Division) eclipsed the North Atlantic Division to become the most literate in the nation. It was a position they held at least until 1930, when illiteracy rates were dropped from the census. [Table 8.4]

Perhaps it was significant, too, that in 1900 the rural states of Nebraska and Iowa (the latter with the most one-room schools in the nation after Illinois) had the highest percentages of literate people ten years of age and older. Kansas, with a majority of its children in one-room schools, followed close behind. Thirty years later, Iowa—still largely rural and still leading all states except heavily urbanized Illinois in the number of one-room schools—continued to have the largest percentage of literate people in the nation. [Illus. 8.10]

Obviously, country schools had accomplished more than outward appearances suggested. How was it possible for children in such seemingly poor schools to have learned to read and write, to have mastered basic arithmetic, and to have tasted the fruits of Western civilization's common literature? What had the experts missed? Certainly they had underestimated the midwestern farmers' interest in educating their children. This would not have been hard to do in many districts, where unpainted schoolhouses and unkempt school yards suggested less than a burning interest in education. But besides this, they could not help but notice that farmers kept their older children out of school when there was farmwork to be done. And finally, educators, like many other observers, may have accepted the idea that

Table 8.4. *Illiterate Population Ten Years of Age and Over, 1880–1930 (%)*

Division	1880	1890	1900	1930
North Atlantic	6.2	6.2	5.9	
South Atlantic	40.3	30.9	23.9	
South Central	39.5	29.7	22.9	
North Central	6.7	5.7	4.2	
Western	11.3	8.3	6.3	
New England				3.7
Middle Atlantic				3.5
East North Central (Midwest)				2.1
West North Central (Midwest)				1.4
South Atlantic				8.3
East South Central				9.6
West South Central				7.2
Mountain				4.2
Pacific				2.1

SOURCE: *Twelfth Census of the United States Taken in the Year 1900: Population, Part II, p. c, and Fifteenth Census of the United States, 1930: Population, Part II, p. 1229.*

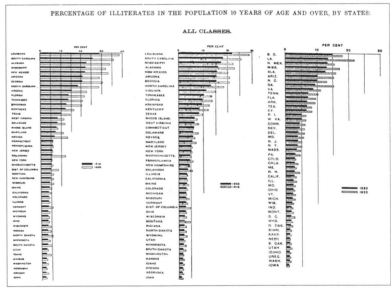

8.10. *In 1900, Nebraska and Iowa—the latter with the most one-room schools in the nation except for Illinois—had the lowest percentage of illiterates in the nation. Thirty years later, Iowa was still the nation's most literate state. (Thirteenth Census of the United States: Population, vol. 1 [Washington, D.C.: GPO, 1913], p. 1202; Fourteenth Census of the United States: Population, vol. 2 [Washington, D.C.: GPO, 1922], p. 1149; Fifteenth Census of the United States: Population, vol. 2 [Washington, D.C.: GPO, 1933], p. 1222)*

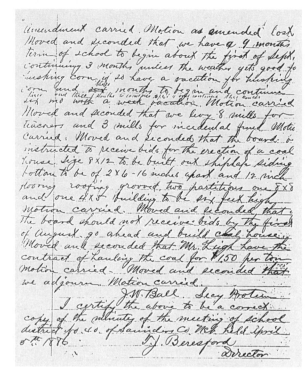

8.11. *In rural one-room schools, farmers set the school terms and designated vacation time for corn-husking. (Dist. No. 40, Saunders Co., Nebr., School Records, NSHS)*

farmers were anti-intellectual and anti-education.

This old notion, which was not without some substance, had been nurtured by nineteenth-century editors of farm papers who charged that farmers were reluctant to accept the principles of scientific agriculture. These accusations may have been fueled by angry editors whose papers the farmers refused to buy. In reality, it was not true that farmers refused to accept new methods of agriculture, only that the value of scientific farming had to be proved to them before they would accept it. Farmers were a practical, common-sense people, skeptical of the speculative and accustomed to embracing what worked. They were much more comfortable with experience than with theories. They would have appreciated and understood John Dickinson's remark at the Constitutional Convention that "experience must be our only guide. *Reason* may mislead us."

Even if their skepticism toward scientific agriculture could be equated with anti-intellectualism, it was no measure of the midwestern farmers' interest in education. They saw education, at least common school education, as a practical necessity. Overall, no people in the nation tried harder or sacrificed more to give their children an elementary education than the midwestern farmers. This was why they built new schoolhouses and added new school apparatus; this was why they sent their children to school long before compulsory education laws said that they must.

The contributions rural parents made to the achievements of their one-room schools cannot be precisely measured; nor can the role of local control in the schools' success be determined with any degree of accuracy. These were intangibles. Yet observers seemed to sense that local control of the schools was important. Even critics of the country schools knew this and gave lip service to it, while attempting to wrest control of the schools from the farmers. "In education as in other departments of human activity," the commissioner of education wrote in 1890, "it is self-help that stimulates the healthiest and most vigorous growth and leads to the most enduring results. . . . History shows conclusively that popular education has flourished most in those States where government is most democratic."

We are so far removed from the control of our schools that it is hard to imagine being personally responsible for what takes place there. We can probably never return—even if we had the will to do so—to small elementary schools governed directly by the public. Indeed, in 1884, one educator who was attempting to emphasize the ridiculousness of small, locally controlled one-room schools suggested they were like having one school for every city block—a catastrophe whose consequences he left to the imagination of his readers.

Nor is it likely that we will ever again have an educational system in which the schools are as much a part of everyday life as they were on the Middle Border in the late nineteenth and early twentieth centuries. In ways peculiarly rural, midwestern country schools were not institutions separate from the busy world; they were as much a part of the rural stream of life as seedtime and harvest. The farmers tended to their fields, to their chores, and to their country schools. They attended school meetings, school programs, and school picnics and arranged their children's education around the rhythms of farm life. Were the children needed at home during cornhusking time? The school schedule made arrangements for this. Was it convenient to remove small children from underfoot during the busiest farm season? They were sent to school for the summer term. Did an infectious disease threaten the health of the children? The country school closed for a time. [Illus. 8.11]

In no place in the land were the elementary schools as closely related to everyday life as they were in the Middle West. Nowhere were the schools controlled to such a great extent by the parents of the children who attended them. Yet these one-room schools were unsatisfactory to those who had been trained to recognize good schools. In the early twentieth century, educators made vigorous efforts to remove these schools from the farmers' control, to make them more efficient, and to shape them in the image of urban schools.

Chapter
9

Rural Renaissance

9.1. *Suffering financially from low farm prices and the effects of the panic of 1893, farmers on the Great Plains joined the Populist party, marched in parades, met in one-room schoolhouses, and demanded help from the government. (KSHS)*

The bells had scarcely stopped ringing the old year out and the new year in on January 1, 1900, before some American opinion makers began writing complacently about the glorious progress the nation had made in the little more than a century of its existence. Others were more interested in predicting the future than reminiscing about the past. One seer foretold the rise of the airplane, others the extensive use of the motorcar; and another imaginative soul speculated that people would one day be shot in tubes from Texas to Georgia. No one, however, predicted the rural renaissance that transformed the nation's heartland between 1900 and World War I.

Only a decade earlier, the rural Midwest—like all of rural America—was almost as isolated as it had been before the Civil War. Country roads were little more than ribbons of dust in summer and impassable ruts in winter. Farmers were still going once or twice a week to get their mail at post offices located several miles from their farms; telephones were virtually unknown; few had even dreamed of modernizing their farm homes.

Worse still, the farmers had been hard hit by the panic of 1893, when corn had sold for fifteen

9.2. *At the beginning of the rural renaissance, the Post Office Department installed new rural free delivery mail routes past farms, churches, and one-room schools, where schoolchildren greeted the mailman. (KSHS)*

9.3. *Delivering farmers' mail and mail-order parcels free to their farms, rural mail carriers broke the grip of rural isolation and country store monopoly.* (World's Work, 28 [June 1914]: 168)

cents a bushel and wheat for twenty-five. Farm foreclosures were widespread, and thousands of angry, frustrated farmers—especially those on the Great Plains—joined the Populist party. They marched in parades across the prairies and congregated in scores of little one-room schoolhouses to charge the government with discrimination and demand the free and unlimited coinage of silver as a means of inflating the currency. [Illus. 9.1] Perhaps their voices were too shrill, their solutions too radical, to attract others caught in the web of the depression. Whatever the reason, their bid to control the government in the 1896 election failed. After that, most of those who had once been zealous campaigners for the people melted back into the parties of their fathers.

Then, as suddenly as clouds gather for a summer shower, prosperity returned to the countryside. And with it came changes that would break the isolation that had held rural America in its grip for so long. Early in the new century, midwestern farm folks began seeing strangers riding past their farms, marking roads on the maps they carried in their buggies. These visitors were postal agents laying out rural free delivery mail routes, which would revolutionize the communication system. In no time at all, the routes were mapped, and rural mail carriers, a new class of government employee, were bringing letters, magazines, and the daily newspaper directly to the farmers' homes free of charge, greeting the

schoolchildren they met along the way. [Illus. 9.2] By 1913, a new parcel post system permitted them to deliver hefty packages from far-away mail-order stores into farmers' mailboxes. So revolutionary was this service that it broke both the express companies' monopoly on package delivery and the country storekeepers' control of the farmers' trade. [Illus. 9.3]

While all this was taking place, another innovation was changing rural life. In more and more places throughout the Midwest, telephone wires—hoisted on poles and stretched along country roads—were carrying the voices of the farmers and their families from farm to farm and from farm to village. No longer did they have to go to town to purchase their necessities. Items could now be ordered from the store by telephone and brought to the farms by the rural mail carriers. [Illus. 9.4]

9.4. *In the new era, telephone poles supporting their message-carrying wires lined country roads, like this one near Antigo, Wisconsin. (Whi [X3] 43026, SHSW)*

9.5. *Rural revival depended on roads. Good-road advocates explained how they would revitalize country life. (Whi [W6] 310, SHSW)*

Industrious farmers, inspired by the need to keep rural post roads in good repair for the mailmen, began grading, ditching, and draining their country roads. Inspired in part by their efforts, a good-roads movement swept the countryside, and in 1916, the national government promised to match the money states spent to build and repair rural post roads. Good roads, proclaimed the movement's posters, meant opportunity for all good things, but poor roads put the family "in a rut." [Illus. 9.5]

No doubt the rural renaissance of the early 1900s owed something to the storm the farmers had raised in the 1890s, but at the root of the rural rebirth were changes taking place in the cities. Until the twentieth century, it had been easy to take rural America for granted and to laugh at hayseeds from the country. The nation had always been rural, and in 1900, more people still lived in rural places than in urban, especially in the Middle West. [Illus. 9.6] But the rapid rise of cities in the closing years of the nineteenth century and the massive exodus of the rural population to urban areas awakened Americans to the realization that old America was swiftly slipping away. One did not need a crystal ball to see that in a few years, more Americans would be living in the cities than in the country—with consequences that no one could foretell.

Those urbanites whose roots lay deep in the soil of the nation's farms and villages regarded this passing of rural America wistfully. A wave of nostalgia for the countryside swept over them as they saw their old America disappearing and realized that the world they had known in their youth would soon be gone. Novelists wrote of rural virtues, and the most popular songs were those like "The Good Old Summer Time," which recalled summer romances in shady country lanes. Even more memorable and certainly more nostalgic was the song "School Days," written in 1907. Ironically, the tune was composed for a vaudeville show by an urban immigrant, and the words were written by a native named Will D. Cobb who was born in Philadelphia, not the rural Midwest! Nevertheless, no song better captured the midwestern one-room school experience or more reminded homesick urbanites of their rural upbringings. [Illus. 9.7]

To many thoughtful Americans, the passing of rural America was more frightening than nostalgic. They had been brought up with the Jeffersonian belief that rural America and its people were the most virtuous part of the state and that cities were the sinkholes of immorality, corruption, crime, and decadence. To them, the depletion of the rural population and the burgeoning of the cities meant disaster for the nation. Was there any way to avert this impending catastrophe?

In that progressive age, when all things seemed possible, President Theodore Roosevelt—one of the concerned—thought so. In 1908, he appointed a commission to find out why farmers were leaving their farms and how country life could be made more attractive to them. The com-

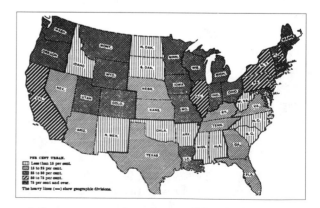

9.6. *In 1900, more Americans still lived on farms and in rural villages than in urban America, especially in the Midwest. (Thirteenth Census of the United States: Population, vol. 1 [Washington, D.C.: GPO, 1913], p. 59)*

mission held hearings around the country, received thousands of answers to its questionnaire, and wrote a sixty-five-page report on its findings. Why did farmers and their children leave the country for the cities? The principal reason, said the commission, was the country school.

Among those the commissioners had questioned were many midwestern educators, who had helped convince them that country schools were bad. It was only natural, therefore, that the educators agreed with the commission that country schools had to be reformed. There was, in fact, little difference between what country and urban children were learning—and that was the trouble. Although country schools taught the basics, they simply did not relate education to country life. Country children, the commission concluded, needed a special "uncitified" curriculum. Its principal recommendation was that rural education be redirected, which meant that every

9.8. *The Country Life Commission—appointed by President Theodore Roosevelt in 1900 to learn why farmers were leaving their farms—blamed the one-room schools and urged the redirection of rural education.* (American School Board Journal 38 [May 1909]: cover)

thing that took place at the schoolhouse, including community gatherings, must be geared toward relating education to country life and keeping farm children on the farm where (presumably) they belonged. [Illus. 9.8]

One step toward that end was to introduce nature study and agriculture into the country school curriculum. If country children were taught these country things, the theory ran, surely they would want to remain in the country. A great campaign was waged by country teachers, county superintendents, college professors, and professionals in the Agriculture Department's Office of Experiment Stations to teach country children about agriculture and the natural world. State courses of study were changed to include agriculture, and the Office of Experiment Stations sent garden seeds to interested groups and issued a small library of helpful bulletins and circulars on teaching agriculture. The crusade reached into nearly every county in the region, stirring hopes and fostering activities designed to keep young people on the farm.

Page County, Iowa, where an enthusiastic young county superintendent threw herself into the task of relating education to country life, was a shining example of what could be done. There, among other projects, young boys were taught to make model farms, and both boys and girls prepared school gardens. [Illus. 9.9] Wherever the new curriculum was introduced, new school apparatus, such as the Babcock milk tester, showed up where only globes, maps, and a dictionary had been before. As practical as the multiplication tables, the milk tester was used by many a proud boy to show his father how much butterfat his cows were producing. [Illus. 9.10]

9.7. *"School Days," composed by an urban immigrant for a vaudeville show, ironically captured the one-room-school experience for nostalgic midwestern urbanites.* (LC)

9.9. Experts believed that in order to keep children on the farm, rural education had to include the study of agriculture. Country children in Page County, Iowa, and elsewhere were taught to make model farms and grow gardens. (U.S. Bureau of Education, Bulletin no. 8 [Washington, D.C.: GPO, 1913], pl. 7)

9.11. Classes in agriculture included instruction in seed testing (top) and corn judging (bottom). (Sixty-fourth Report of the Public Schools of the State of Missouri: School Year Ending June 30, 1913 [Jefferson City, n.d.], opp. p. 48)

9.10. In schools like this one near Chokio, Minnesota, new school apparatus such as the Babcock milk tester was needed where charts, maps, and dictionaries had once sufficed. (U.S. Bureau of Education, Bulletin no. 8 [Washington, D.C.: GPO, 1913], pl. 6)

Teaching agriculture was more important in some counties than in others, of course. Much depended on the county superintendents. If they embraced the new curriculum, they saw to it that their schools included courses in agriculture. In some schools, this meant training in seed testing and corn judging as well as the use of the Babcock milk tester. [Illus. 9.11] But that was only the beginning. Even before 4-H clubs were organized, county superintendents helped their teachers organize farm clubs whose members undertook various projects, such as raising corn or sewing. Among the most popular of these were the pig clubs, which, as war began in Europe in 1914, were supported and publicized by the Department of Agriculture. [Illus. 9.12]

Through the long hot summers, club members

9.12. *Before 4-H clubs were organized, county superintendents helped teachers form various kinds of farm clubs. With the outbreak of war in Europe in 1914, the Department of Agriculture promoted the formation of pig clubs among the nation's youth. (Yearbook of the United States Department of Agriculture, 1915 [Washington, D.C.: GPO, 1916], pl. 22)*

9.14. *Competition among eighth-grade farm boys extended to plowing contests near Lamberton, Minnesota, before World War I. (Minn. State Dept. of Education)*

9.13. *Country schoolchildren displayed their work at state and county fairs, where they competed for prizes. (Sixty-third Report of the Public Schools of the State of Missouri: School Year Ending June 30, 1912 [Jefferson City, n.d.], p. 257)*

worked on their projects, inspired by the prospect of rewards at the end of the growing season. In the fall, they entered the fruits of their labor in county and state fairs, where they competed for prizes. [Illus. 9.13] Competition, that lifeblood of Americans, did not end with the best pig or the best dress; it extended to corn raising, livestock judging, and even plowing contests. Not long before the outbreak of World War I, one such contest was photographed near Lamberton, Minnesota, where a group of eighth-grade students plowed furrows and lined up in their Sunday clothes to have their picture taken. [Illus. 9.14]

These clubs and the competitions that went with them unquestionably generated excitement among farm children, but were they enough to keep country children on the farm? Some leaders thought not. With seemingly the whole world moving cityward and urbanites regarding country people as inferior beings, it was clear that rural children must be taught to love the country and to value their own worth. For this purpose, various creeds—one for boys and one for girls—were written and given to the children to memorize. [Illus. 9.15]

Finally, of course, the success of the redirection of rural education depended on country teachers. But teaching agriculture—like bilingual education in our own time—was something new, and teachers had to be trained. Consequently, county institutes and normal schools put in a lot

A Country Girl's Creed
BY JESSIE FIELD

I AM GLAD I live in the country. I love its beauty and its spirit. I rejoice in the things I can do as a country girl for my home and my neighborhood.

I believe I can share in the beauty around me—in the fragrance of the orchards in spring, in the bending wheat at harvest time, in the morning song of birds, and in the glow of the sunset on the far horizon. I want to express this beauty in my own life as naturally and happily as the wild rose blooms by the roadside.

I believe I can have a part in the courageous spirit of the country. This spirit has entered into the brook in our pasture. The stones placed in its way call forth its strength and add to its strength a song. It dwells in the tender plants as they burst the seed-cases that imprison them and push through the dark earth to the light. It sounds in the nesting notes of the meadow-lark. With this courageous spirit I too can face the hard things of life with gladness.

I believe there is much I can do in my country home. Through studying the best way to do my every-day work, I can find joy in common tasks done well. Through loving comradeship I can help bring into my home the happiness and peace that are always so near us in God's out-of-door world. Through such a home I can help make real to all who pass that way their highest ideal of country life.

I believe my love and loyalty for my country home should reach out in service to that larger home that we call our neighborhood. I would join with the people who live there in true friendliness. I would whole-heartedly give my best to further all that is being done for a better community. I would have all that I think and say and do help to unite country people, near and far, in that great Kingdom of Love for neighbors which the Master came to establish—the Master who knew and cared for country ways and country folks.

COMPLIMENTS OF
SUPT. E. M. RAPP

9.15. *To strengthen their self-image and love of the country, rural boys and girls in the Midwest memorized creeds emphasizing the beauty of the country and community service. (SHSI, Iowa City, Agnes Samuelson Collection)*

of time and effort training country teachers how to teach this new subject and relate rural education to rural life. Their training closely followed the new theory of "learning by doing," and student teachers—dressed more appropriately for the classroom than for the field—were sent out to hoe in the normal school gardens. Others were taught to build wooden structures for use in developing this new thing called "vitalized agriculture." [Illus. 9.16] At some county institutes, country teachers—both male and female—were taught the rudiments of livestock judging. [Illus. 9.17]

The teaching of agriculture in one-room schools never developed as the theorists intended, however. By and large, country teachers disliked teaching agriculture. Some resented teaching what they considered a nonacademic subject, and others thought that teaching agriculture to country children was like carrying coal to Newcastle. More than that, the teachers saw it as just one more subject for them to be tested in. Their lack of enthusiasm showed up in their teaching. Much to the disgust of the educators, most teachers taught agriculture perfunctorily from pamphlets or textbooks. They rarely engaged the children in hands-on projects, as the theorists had intended, through which the students could learn arithmetic, geography, and all the other common branches of learning while relating the entire curriculum to country life.

More enthusiasm for the study of nature and the rudiments of agriculture was displayed in urban schools. There, nature walks through the parks became part of many city school programs, and school gardens were planted in city lots. Where there was no room for real gardens, window gardens—planted with seed supplied by the Office of Experiment Stations—hung from

Left: 9.16. Learning how to teach agriculture and related subjects occupied some of the teachers' time at the normal schools and county institutes. (Top: Twentieth Biennial Report of the Nebraska State Superintendent of Public Instruction, 1907–1908 [Lincoln, 1909], opp. p. 271; bottom: Sixty-eighth Report of the Public Schools of the State of Missouri: School Year Ending June 30, 1917 [Jefferson City, n.d.], p. 334)

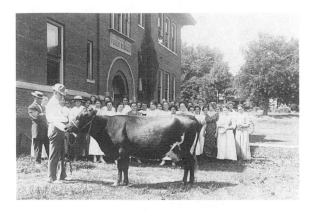

9.17. *Both male and female country teachers were occasionally taught the rudiments of livestock judging.* (SHSI, Iowa City, Huftalen Collection)

9.18. *Condemned schoolhouse. Wisconsin school authorities condemned some one-room schoolhouses in the early 1900s, leaving farmers no choice but to build new ones.* (Fourteenth Biennial Report of the Wisconsin Superintendent of Public Instruction, 1908–1910 *[Madison, 1910], p. 13*)

countless city schoolrooms. Here, children who did not live every day with growing things could see the marvels of nature.

The redirection of rural education encompassed more than teaching agriculture and organizing farm clubs. The more visible and significant part of the great effort to uplift the rural Midwest was the building of new one-room schools. Since the end of the Civil War, the status of midwestern farmers' prosperity could more or less be measured by the condition of their schoolhouses. When times were bad, the schoolhouses were neglected; when they were good, farmers often built new schoolhouses. Through the years, they had gone from log and sod schoolhouses to plain schoolhouses and finally to improved school buildings. In the prosperous 1900s, they began building once more.

In some places, they had no choice. By 1910, Wisconsin school officials had been given the authority by the state legislature to condemn dangerous school buildings. This, in itself, was a sign of the times. In the past, the state legislature would no more have sanctioned such a practice than it would have eliminated the small, independent school districts. In any case, when the officials acted—as they did from time to time—the farmers had no choice but to build anew. [Illus. 9.18]

Most of the time, however, the farmers decided on their own—as they had always done—to build new schoolhouses. Sometimes the new schools were the third or fourth ones they had

built, and in those golden years before World War I, many of the old buildings—like that in District No. 3 in Fillmore County, Nebraska—were torn down to make way for the new. [Illus. 9.19] In Ford County, Kansas, the old schoolhouse stood side by side with the new one for a time, perhaps eliciting mixed feelings among the farmers. For what person who had attended the little school could help feeling a tinge of sadness at its passing? Yet the new school also signified progress, and only the district crank would want to stand in its way. [Illus. 9.20]

The new schoolhouses were, in their own way, symbols of the rural renaissance. For the first time, school officials were able to persuade farmers who were building new schoolhouses to follow the designs of architects—who reaped a rich harvest drawing country schoolhouses in those years. With bold imagination, they turned the plain one-room structures into buildings that farm folks scarcely recognized as schoolhouses.

Consider the beautiful sketch of a schoolhouse drawn for a rural district in Minnesota, for example. Aside from the startling departure from the rectangular box design of an earlier day, one of the principal features of this building was, as the architect explained, its expansibility. If necessary, another room could easily be added. [Illus. 9.21] Or take the new school in District No. 21

DISTRICT SCHOOL No. 3, FILLMORE COUNTY
This building was destroyed to make room for—

The New School Building in
DISTRICT No. 3, FILLMORE COUNTY

9.19. During the rural renaissance, new and architecturally different one-room schoolhouses replaced the old ones in many school districts. Old and new schoolhouses in District No. 3, Fillmore County, Nebraska. (Seventeenth Biennial Report of the Nebraska State Superintendent of Public Instruction, 1901–1902 [Lincoln, 1903], p. 387)

Right: 9.22. The schoolhouse in District No. 21, Boone County, Nebraska, exemplified one kind of country schoolhouse built during the Midwest's rural revival. (Twenty-third Biennial Report of the Nebraska State Superintendent of Public Instruction, 1913–1915 [Lincoln, 1916], opp. p. 208)

in Boone County, Nebraska. An excellent example of the Midwest's rural revival, it marked another milestone in the homesteaders' progress from pioneers to prosperous settled citizens. It cost $2,000, and its floor plan revealed two porches—one open and one closed—a separate

9.20. In Ford County, Kansas, old and new schoolhouses stood side by side for a time, eliciting both nostalgic memories and hopes for the future. (Twenty-first Biennial Report of the State Superintendent of Public Instruction of Kansas, for the Years Ending June 30, 1917, and June 30, 1918 [Topeka, 1918], p. 20)

9.21. Built from architects' plans in the early 1900s, new midwestern schoolhouses were distinctive symbols of the rural renaissance. (Minn. State Dept. of Education)

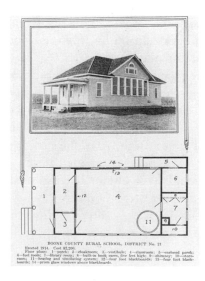

BOONE COUNTY RURAL SCHOOL, DISTRICT No. 21
Erected 1914. Cost $2,200.

library, and a cloakroom that was separate from the vestibule, where the children had always hung their coats and caps before. [Illus. 9.22]

9.23. *Porches—like this one in District No. 21, Jackson County, Minnesota—were a distinguishing feature of one-room schoolhouses built in the progressive years. (Minn. State Dept. of Education)*

These were only two of the numerous designs farmers followed in constructing their schoolhouses in the new era. Porches—like the four-pillared affair on the schoolhouse built in 1910 in District No. 21, Jackson County, Minnesota—became as distinguishable a feature of midwestern rural school architecture in the early 1900s as Doric pillars had been during the Greek revival. [Illus. 9.23] But they were not all alike. The architect who tinkered with the Boston School in District No. 62, Lyon County, Kansas, in 1912—as the rural rebirth movement neared its zenith—designed a porch whose roof uniquely covered

9.24. *Architects devised various kinds of porches and cloakrooms for new schoolhouses. Boston School, District No. 62, Lyon County, Kansas. (Walter M. Anderson Collection, Emporia, Kans.)*

9.25. *Resembling the belfry on older schoolhouses, the tower of the new Crossroads Schoolhouse in Macon County, Illinois, was all that distinguished it from a home. (U.S. Bureau of Education, Bulletin no. 12 [Washington, D.C.: GPO, 1914], pl. 1)*

both the girls' and boys' cloakrooms. [Illus. 9.24]

No one was likely to mistake either of these one-room schoolhouses for some other kind of building. The same could not be said, however, for the Crossroads Schoolhouse near Decatur in Macon County, Illinois. Constructed in 1911 at a cost of $2,500, it was the fifth schoolhouse built in the district's eighty-year history. The architect who designed this schoolhouse obviously labored to make it different. No pillared porch shaded its front doors; a covered entry, flanked by two windows, led through double doors into a vestibule and past swinging doors into the classroom. Only the flag-flying tower, resembling the belfries on older schools, distinguished this building from a home. [Illus. 9.25].

The interior of the Crossroads Schoolhouse differed little from that of Nebraska's Boone County school. Entering the classroom through the vestibule's swinging doors, the boys turned left and the girls right to reach their respective cloakrooms, both of which were within the teacher's view. Beyond the girls' cloakroom was the library. Small but separate from the classroom, it was ideal for a country school. [Illus. 9.26]

Common to most new schoolhouses of the period—and a certain sign of the rural revival—were banks of windows replacing the three or four that had been standard on each side of the old schoolhouses. The architects' consensus seemed to be that lighting had been the worst feature of the old one-room schoolhouses, and they

9.26. *Entering the schoolroom of the Crossroads Schoolhouse through swinging doors, boys turned left and girls turned right to reach their respective cloakrooms. Adjacent to the girls' cloakroom was the school library. (U.S. Bureau of Education, Bulletin no. 12 [Washington, D.C.: GPO, 1914], pl. 23)*

9.28. *"Unilateral lighting"—emitting light into the Crossroads Schoolhouse through a bank of windows on the students' left—was an innovation in one-room school architecture during the rural renaissance. (U.S. Bureau of Education, Bulletin no. 12 [Washington, D.C.: GPO, 1914], pl. 22)*

were determined to make up for years of poor illumination. Minnesota's Plan No. 7 for rural schoolhouses was a good example of the architects' fondness for light during the rural renaissance. This plan featured four large windows grouped closely together, occupying a large part of each side of the building. [Illus. 9.27] But there were other ways to bring more light into the classroom. At the Crossroads Schoolhouse, the outside light entered the classroom principally through one bank of windows on the students' left, since most were right-handed. The architects

9.27. *This schoolhouse in District No. 41, Pine County, Minnesota, features banks of windows on each side of the building. It was built according to the state's Plan No. 7 and cost $1,632. (Minn. State Dept. of Education)*

even had a name for this arrangement: "unilateral lighting." [Illus. 9.28]

The new schools were expensive compared with the old, many of them running to $2,000 or more. But farmers who wished to build for less had various models to choose from. The model country school built in 1907 on the campus of Western State Normal in Hays, Kansas, showed how an excellent school could be built for under $2,000. Besides the main cloakroom, this small building contained two other cloakrooms, two closets, and two toilets. For vocational subjects, which were just becoming popular in the country, the schoolhouse had an annex where manual training and domestic science could be taught. If the indoor toilets were omitted, the schoolhouse could be built for about $1,750. [Illus. 9.29] The effort to keep the building's cost below $2,000 probably accounted for the omission of a basement, which was a feature of one-room schoolhouses whose time had come. The new Crossroads Schoolhouse had one, as did Minnesota's Plan No. 7 and many others being built in the new era.

One of the most elaborate and most publicized of all the model country schools used to train teachers in the Midwest was the one built on the campus of the Kirksville State Normal School in the early 1900s. [Illus. 9.30] Among other things,

9.29. *This model schoolhouse on the campus of Western State Normal in Hays, Kansas, could be built for $1,750 if the indoor toilets were omitted. (Seventeenth Biennial Report of the State Superintendent of Public Instruction of Kansas, for the Years Ending June 30, 1909, and June 30, 1910 [Topeka, 1910], p. 53)*

9.30. *The model school at Kirksville State Normal in Kirksville, Missouri, was perhaps the most elaborate and most publicized of those used to train country teachers. (Pickler Memorial Library, NE Mo. State Univ.)*

this building illustrated just how useful a basement could be. It contained a coal room, a room for storage of flower bulbs, a darkroom, and a gymnasium. One of the basement's most important functions, however, was to house the furnace that heated the entire school and provided hot water. On the upper floor, there were indoor toilets and showers for girls and boys in addition to the large schoolroom and library. One school official argued that it demonstrated "the fact that a rural school can have all the sanitary and other conveniences enjoyed by any city school." But of course, this model school was only a dream illustrating the expansiveness of progressive thought. Few, if any, small, independent school districts could afford such elaborate facilities, which had cost more than $12,000 to build. [Illus. 9.31] Nor did they need to.

Those schools that could afford a basement like the one in the Crossroads Schoolhouse found that it provided room for community activities

Right: 9.31. The basement of the model school at Kirksville Normal provided space for a furnace and a gymnasium. The upper floor contained girls' and boys' showers, which some thought were especially needed for farm children. (U.S. Bureau of Education, Bulletin no. 12 [Washington, D.C.: GPO, 1914], pp. 112–13)

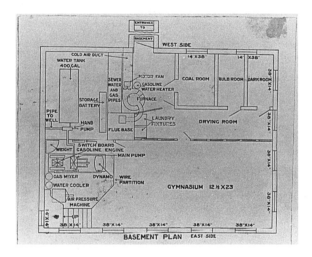

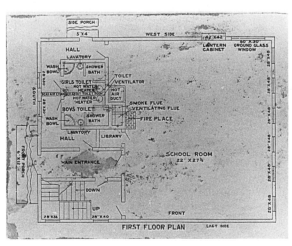

and allowed the big stove in the classroom to be replaced with a furnace. This alone was enough to make the basement a great advance in one-room school construction. Still, not many districts could afford a furnace, to say nothing of a basement. Most were forced to keep the big stove someplace in the classroom as they had always done. And in far too many schoolrooms, a visitor on a winter's day was likely to find the little room buttoned up tight and the children breathing air that had grown stale with overuse. [Illus. 9.32]

Even so, in the more prosperous districts, the big stove was likely to be different from the old monster that made it too warm for children near it, too cold for those farther away, and tended to fill the room with fetid air. In those progressive, innovative days, numerous farmers found a better way to heat their children's schoolrooms. They purchased a new kind of jacketed stove that drew fresh air from outside and sent it down an air shaft between the jacket and the stove, where it was heated and passed into the room. Eventually the fetid air found its way back to the outside through another pipe so that the air was continually circulating. [Illus. 9.33]

9.33. *During the rural renaissance, districts that could afford them installed new jacketed stoves, which carried fresh air into the schoolroom and removed the old. (U.S. Bureau of Education, Bulletin no. 8 [Washington, D.C.: GPO, 1913], pl. 5)*

The new schoolhouses designed by architects were not for every district, of course, as a host of midwesterners who attended country schools between the two world wars can attest. Thousands of districts could not afford them, and many plain one-room schools built as early as the 1870s continued to serve until after the Great Depression, when they closed forever. Yet in the spring and summer of those years when the century was still young, farmers almost everywhere were eagerly improving their old schoolhouses and beautifying their school yards. It was as if they really believed that doing so would help keep their children on the farm and save rural America.

One such school became famous as a model for rebuilding an entire community through the redirection of rural education. The Porter School in District No. 3, Adair County, Missouri, was some three miles north of Kirksville. In 1912, the schoolhouse, like the district itself, was in deplorable shape. In fifteen years, it had never been repaired. Without any visible foundation, it sat flat on the ground; some of its shutters had been torn off, and the grounds around it were without trees or shrubs. [Illus. 9.34] Its interior had been equally neglected. Plaster had fallen from the walls, and the wallpaper was torn and dirty. No curtains or even shades covered the windows. An old stove stood in the center of the

9.32. *Country school districts that could afford neither a basement to house a furnace nor a new stove struggled on through World War I with the traditional heating arrangement, which brought no fresh air into the classroom on cold winter days. (U.S. Bureau of Education, Bulletin no. 8 [Washington, D.C.: GPO, 1913], pl. 5)*

9.34. *In early 1912, the Porter School in District No. 3, Adair County, Missouri, had already been neglected for more than fifteen years. It had no foundation beneath it, a shutter was torn from one window, and weeds had grown up beside it. (Sixty-sixth Report of the Public Schools of the State of Missouri: School Year Ending June 1915 [Jefferson City, n.d.], opp. p. 32)*

room; its stovepipe—dark with soot—ran along the ceiling to the chimney. [Illus. 9.35] Tramps had taken the door to the girls' privy to build a fire. [Illus. 9.36] So forlorn was the school that a number of the district's farmers would not allow their children to attend there. Instead, they sent them—usually by wagon—to the model country school on the Kirksville State Normal campus. [Illus. 9.37]

That same year, however, Marie Harvey Turner, a vigorous woman who taught at the model country school at Kirksville State Normal, resigned her position to become the teacher at the Porter School. Her purpose was to demonstrate how the redirection of rural education could revivify an entire rural community. It was the act of a dedicated, confident crusader who reflected the very heart of progressivism. Only a true believer would have given up her status as a normal school professor to become the teacher of a broken-down one-room school. Almost overnight she revitalized the dying community. At her insistence and under her direction, a basement was built beneath the schoolhouse. Besides giving the schoolhouse a solid foundation, it provided a place for a furnace, sink, and water supply, as well as a room for community activities. This room was in such demand during the week that scheduling its use became a problem. [Illus. 9.38] In the main room, the stove was removed, the walls were replastered and repapered, window shades were hung, and the room was beautifully

9.35. *The interior of the Porter School—marred by dirty walls, torn wallpaper, and a blackened stovepipe—matched its neglected exterior. (U.S. Bureau of Education, Bulletin no. 12 [Washington, D.C.: GPO, 1914], pl. 30)*

decorated. [Illus. 9.39] Meanwhile, the barren school grounds were being transformed. In time, the privies were repaired and screened, playground equipment was purchased, a flagpole was erected, and a horse barn was constructed. The community's renewed care and concern for the

9.36. *The girls' privy at the Porter School reflected the farmers' general neglect of their school. (U.S. Bureau of Education, Bulletin no. 12 [Washington, D.C.: GPO, 1914], pl. 29)*

9.37. *The dismal condition of the Porter School caused some farmers in the district to wagon their children to the model school at Kirksville State Normal. (U.S. Bureau of Education, Bulletin no. 30 [Washington, D.C.: GPO, 1914], pl. 8)*

9.39. *The Porter School classroom was repapered and handsomely decorated. (Sixty-sixth Report of the Public Schools of the State of Missouri: School Year Ending 1915 [Jefferson City, n.d.], opp. p. 33)*

school were apparent in the trees, shrubs, and rosebushes that graced the front of the schoolhouse not long after World War I. [Illus. 9.40]

The Porter School may have been the most famous midwestern school around which country life was reinvigorated during the rural renaissance, but it was not the only one. In places such as Page County, Iowa, and Winnebago County, Illinois, energetic county superintendents won national acclaim for revitalizing schools and rural life in their counties.

At the same time, midwestern farmers—spurred by the reformers' enthusiasm for rebuilding the rural Midwest and keeping country chil-

dren on the farm—were caught up in a campaign to develop standard schools. It is not known who first thought of creating standard schools, but the idea spread quickly across the region. The educators led the way, establishing a list of requirements a district had to fulfill to have a standard school. And once again, that old competitive drive among farmers and their districts hastened the development of such schools. By 1914, standard schools or their equivalent could be found in one district or another throughout the Midwest.

The requirements for a standard school varied from state to state, but to qualify, a school generally had to employ a teacher with a certificate above the third-grade level, pay him or her a certain salary, have a library of so many volumes, hold school for so many months, and maintain a clean, sanitary schoolhouse. In most states, any school that met such requirements was awarded some kind of recognition. In Michigan, it was a plaque that could be attached to the outside of the schoolhouse. Often it was hung above the front door, where it could be seen by everyone entering the building and by passersby too. The plaque was a mark of distinction. Like the big bell, it made one country school different from another and gave the district's people the right to be proud of their school's superiority. [Illus. 9.41]

To urban sophisticates, this achievement may have been too trivial to notice, but to small mid-

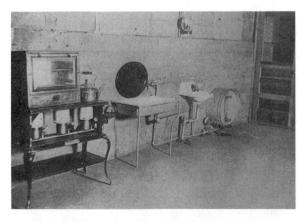

9.38. *Renovation of the Porter School in 1912 included a basement containing an indoor water supply, a furnace, a cookstove, and a community room (not shown). (Sixty-sixth Report of the Public Schools of the State of Missouri: School Year Ending 1915 [Jefferson City, n.d.], opp. p. 33)*

9.40. *In time, the farmers beautified the Porter School's barren school grounds with trees and shrubbery and built a shed for horses. (Pickler Memorial Library, NE Mo. State Univ.)*

9.41. *To help promote the rural uplift movement, midwestern states awarded "standard school" certificates and plaques to one-room schools that met certain basic requirements. District No. 1, Muskegon County, Michigan. (Seventy-seventh Annual Report of the Superintendent of Public Instruction of the State of Michigan, 1913–1914 [Lansing, 1914], portfolio of standard schools)*

western school districts, winning the plaque was a mark of excellence to be treasured and celebrated. No account accompanied the photograph of those who gathered under the trees for the standard school award ceremony in District No. 3, Big Prairie Township, Newaygo County, Michigan, in 1913. But it was clear from the Sunday clothes they wore that they regarded this as an important occasion and considered the plaque—for which they had made so many sacrifices—a major step in the progress of their community. [Illus. 9.42]

Just as the big bell and belfry had reflected the midwestern farmers' aspirations for their children and communities, so did standard schools, whose numbers multiplied just before World War I. By the end of the war, Kansas had nearly five hundred such schools. Some of them were like the Lincoln School on the dry plains of Finney County, where a windmill supplied the water for the new school. [Illus. 9.43]

New schoolhouses, standard schools, and the teaching of nature and agriculture were all very well, but for professional educators, these innovations were not enough to make good schools. No matter how beautiful the new rural renaissance schoolhouses might be, they were still controlled by inefficient, cantankerous school boards and farmers. According to the authorities, until this was corrected, country schools would never amount to much. For years, midwestern educators had been attempting to change the rural schools. And although they had succeeded

in a number of ways, their efforts to convince state legislatures to let them wrest control of the schools from the farmers had failed.

Now, in the fervor to rebuild rural America, they renewed their efforts to remold rural education in the image of urban schools. Through the years, educational experts had advocated making an entire township one school district, thereby eliminating the school boards of the six or seven schools in the township. According to this plan, one school board or one director would suffice for the entire township. Indiana had such a system, and Iowa had a mixed system of township districts and small, independent districts. But most state legislatures would no more eliminate the small districts than they would vote for higher taxes, and thus the old system continued throughout most of the Midwest.

9.42. *The importance farmers attached to winning a "standard school" plaque is suggested by this dressed-up gathering celebrating the award in District No. 3, Big Prairie Township, Newaygo County, Michigan, in 1913. (Seventy-seventh Annual Report of the Superintendent of Public Instruction of the State of Michigan, 1913–1914 [Lansing, 1914], portfolio of standard schools)*

9.43. *In 1918, Kansas had almost five hundred standard schools. One, the Lincoln School in Finney County, on the western Kansas plains, had its own windmill to supply its water.* (Twenty-first Biennial Report of the State Superintendent of Public Instruction of Kansas, 1917–1918 [Topeka, 1918], p. 21)

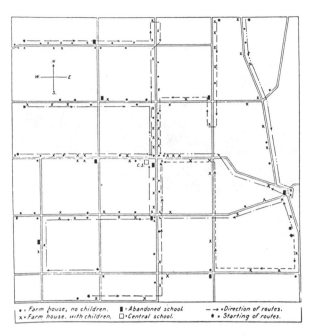

•• *Farm house, no children.* ▮ *=Abandoned school.* — → =*Direction of routes.*
x = *Farm house, with children.* ☐ =*Central school.* • = *Starting of routes.*

9.45. *This map shows the routes the wagons followed to bring children to the Gustavus Consolidated School and the schools eliminated by consolidation.* (Report of the U.S. Commissioner of Education for the Year 1900–01 [Washington, D.C.: GPO, 1902), p. 167)

Stymied in their efforts to create township districts, midwestern educators had a better idea in the era of rural uplift. Why not, they asked, consolidate three or four small schools into one big one? Where the distance to the consolidated schoolhouse was too far for some children to walk, the district could wagon them to school. This idea had already surfaced in the 1890s in Ohio and Indiana, where several consolidations had been made. The Gustavus School in Gustavus Township, Gustavus County, Ohio, was one of the pioneers. It was built in 1898 at a cost

9.44. *The Gustavus Consolidated School in Gustavus Township, Gustavus County, Ohio, was built in 1898, at the start of the consolidation movement. It cost $3,000 and eliminated nine small schools.* (OHS)

of $3,000 and was set in the open country, where, as one observer put it, "country life was being preserved." It had four rooms, a principal, and three assistants. It eliminated nine small schools and drew some 186 children, including those in high school, from homes scattered over an area twenty-five miles square. [Illus. 9.44] To bring these isolated children to school, the district secured the use of nine wagons and employed nine drivers. Each driver was paid an average of $1.25 a day and had a specified route that permitted him to pick up every child at the gate of his or her father's farm. [Illus. 9.45] Every possible problem appeared to have been foreseen and resolved. Even the children's comfort in bitter weather had been planned for by equipping the wagons with curtains, soapstones, and lap robes. [Illus. 9.46]

Here, at last, was the perfect answer to the rural school problem. One observer wrote: "Anyone who stands in that building [Gustavus Consolidated] and looks at those children and wagons, must be convinced that here is the solution

9.46. *For the children's comfort in winter, school wagons used by consolidated schools were equipped with curtains, soapstones, and lap robes. (OHS)*

9.47. *Pictured are four of the nine wagons that transported children to the new Gustavus Consolidated School in the early 1900s. "Anyone who . . . looks at those children and wagons," an observer wrote," must be convinced that here is the solution of the country-school problem." (OHS)*

of the country-school problem, because this problem is being solved in the country over 6 miles from the nearest railroad." [Illus. 9.47] Not until the fever to save rural America mounted and the redirection of rural education became a slogan during the rural Midwest's Indian summer, however, was consolidation widely acclaimed as the answer to the rural school problem. Then, in state after state, superintendents of public instruction began filling their annual reports with the wonders of what consolidation would do for rural education. In 1903, in a speech given at the National Education Association convention, the state superintendent of Nebraska listed twenty-nine arguments for consolidation and only twelve against. [Illus. 9.48] These were such logical arguments that they seemed irrefutable. What parent would not want his or her child to go to a larger, finer school, to have a better teacher, to be challenged by more students, or to ride to school in a wagon? Even the American belief that "bigger is better" and the theory of evolution, which measured progress by movement from the simple to the complex, were on the side of consolidation.

"Consolidation" became the new catchword for the reform of midwestern rural schools, and the movement spread virtually nonstop through Ohio and Indiana. In Indiana, especially, hundreds of small schools slipped swiftly into the maw of centralization. Was this because Indiana farmers cared less or more about their children's education than those in other midwestern states?

No one knew for certain. Outwardly, at least, it appeared that they cared more. Still, the farmers in Indiana, where the township system of education prevailed, had been less involved in the day-to-day operation of their one-room schools than those in any other midwestern state. Perhaps they merely cared less about the mechanics of education than did other midwestern farmers, who were accustomed to running their own schools. Whatever the reason, 181 wagons were already carrying 2,599 Indiana schoolchildren to consolidated schools by 1902, and in some instances, whole townships had already been consolidated. Every schoolchild in Wayne County's Webster Township, for example, was attending school in the town of Webster. And nearly everywhere across the state, people were talking about consolidation, planning new schoolhouses, and making preparations for wagoning children to school.

In the summer of 1901, the people in Union

Arguments for Consolidation

1. It insures a much larger per cent of enumerated pupils enrolled.
2. Reduces irregular attendance.
3. Prevents tardiness among transported pupils.
4. Pupils can be better classified and graded.
5. No wet feet or clothing, nor colds resulting therefrom.
6. No quarreling, improper language, or improper conduct on the way to and from school.
7. Pupils are under the care of responsible persons from the time they leave home in the morning until they return at night.
8. Pupils can have the advantage of better school rooms, better heated, better ventilated, and better supplied with apparatus, etc.
9. Pupils have the advantage of that interest, enthusiasm and confidence which large classes always bring.
10. Better teachers can be employed, hence better schools.
11. The plan insures more thorough and more complete supervision.
12. It is more economical. Under the new plan the cost of tuition per pupil on the basis of total enrollment has been reduced from $16.00 to $10.48; on the basis of average attendance, from $26.66 to $16.07. This statement is for pupils in subdistricts Nos. 10 and 13, Lake county, Ohio.

9.48. *Here are some of the twenty-nine arguments the Nebraska superintendent of public instruction listed in favor of consolidation. (Eighteenth Biennial Report of the Nebraska State Superintendent of Public Instruction, 1904 [York, 1905], p. 227)*

9.49. *The consolidated school in Union Township, Montgomery County, Indiana, had four rooms, two furnaces, and cost $12,000, but it eliminated four one-room schools.* (Twenty-first Biennial Report of the State Superintendent of Public Instruction, Indiana, 1901–1902 *[Indianapolis, 1903], p. 743)*

Township, Montgomery County, built an imposing consolidated schoolhouse in the open country on two acres of ground. It had four rooms, two large halls, and a basement. Not one but two coal furnaces heated the new building. It cost $12,000 to build but took the place of four one-room schools. Two wagons brought the children to school, and no child had to ride farther than five miles. [Illus. 9.49] Not all of Indiana's early consolidated schools were as large, however. The schoolhouse in Bloomfield Township, Lagrange County, appeared to be about half the size of the one in Union. Yet it required the same number of wagons to haul the children to school. [Illus. 9.50]

These consolidations were accompanied by glowing reports of their success. Letters of support from patrons were solicited by the Indiana superintendent of public instruction and published; papers arguing the advantages of consolidation appeared in the education journals; and popular magazines ran a number of articles on the remaking of rural America. In their enthusiasm for consolidation, however, supporters apparently forgot that the purpose of redirecting rural education was to make it different from urban education in order to keep farm children on the farm. Instead, they were actually making rural schools as much like city schools as possible. Besides that, one of the aims of the rural planners had been to restore and rebuild the lives

of rural communities. But the loss of one-room schools through consolidation meant the end of many little communities, whose lives had centered around their schools.

Nevertheless, on the wings of the favorable publicity surrounding it, consolidation moved ahead. Impressed by its apparent success, some state legislatures enacted laws offering farmers financial inducements to consolidate their schools. Minnesota, for example, lured the farmers with the promise of help in building new consolidated schoolhouses. For some small districts in need of better schools, this offer was too good to reject. By World War I, it was not uncommon to find several weather-beaten one-room schools that had once nurtured hundreds of farm children forsaken for one big consolidated school. [Illus. 9.51] One such consolidation occurred in Thomson Township, Carlton County, Minnesota. In terms of the number of wagons necessary to transport children to school, this was a large consolidation. It came just at the dawn of the auto age; three of the conveyances used to take the children to and from the schoolhouse were motorized. [Illus. 9.52]

With all the fervor and publicity accompanying consolidation, one might have thought that midwestern farmers were eager to have their one-room schools absorbed into larger ones. But other than in Ohio and Indiana and a few scat-

9.50. *Though small, this consolidated school in Bloomfield Township, Lagrange County, Indiana, still required two wagons to transport the children to school.* (Twenty-first Biennial Report of the State Superintendent of Public Instruction, Indiana, 1901–1902 *[Indianapolis, 1903], p. 759)*

tered places in other states, this was not so. Actually, most farmers opposed consolidation as vigorously as they had opposed township districts, and their reasons for doing so were as logical to them as the arguments for consolidation were to the educators.

The truth was that consolidation never really lived up to its advocates' claims. For example, early promoters of the system marveled at the efficiency of the drivers who carried the children to and from school in their wagons. They gave almost eloquent accounts of how the children were picked up at their front gates, the drivers' regularity assuring that no child ever had to stand shivering in the cold. No more wet feet, they said; no more colds; no more tardiness; and no more bullying of the younger children by the older ones on the way to school. They told how carefully the drivers had been selected, how they had contracted to prohibit the children from swearing or using obscene language, and how they had agreed not to smoke or permit any child to do so. All told, the climate aboard the hacks appeared to be as pure as that of the children's homes.

To hear the advocates tell it, the system was as efficient as it was successful. And indeed, photographs of large schoolhouses and the hundred or so children ready to board the wagons for the pleasant ride home—even if used for propaganda

9.52. *The number of vehicles necessary to transport children to this consolidated schoolhouse near the dawn of the auto age signaled the beginning of big schools in the rural Midwest. Washington School, Thomson Township, Carlton County, Minnesota. (Minn. State Dept. of Education)*

purposes—seemed to prove the argument. [Illus. 9.53] But it turned out that neither the drivers nor the wagons were all that satisfactory. Even in Lagrange County, Indiana, where an early consolidation had been lavishly praised, a poll indicated that some farmers were less than enchanted with the new system. Some 14 percent indicated that the driver did not come by every day; 21 percent complained that the conveyance was not on time; and 32 percent said that the vehicle was uncomfortable. More than 22 percent said that the team was too slow, and 17 percent thought that the driver was not responsible.

Part of the trouble, of course, was the roads. In spite of the good-roads movement, most country roads were still dirt and subject to all the evils thereof. To expect anyone to drive a wagon along a five-mile route over snow-covered roads in winter and muddy ruts in spring and stay on schedule was to expect a miracle. [Illus. 9.54] More troublesome was the expense. As consolidation was tried in more and more places, it was found to be too expensive to pass by each farm in the district. The result was that a number of children had to walk some distance to catch the hack. For the same reason, responsible drivers could not always be employed. Some consolidated districts turned to teenagers or other less responsible people to drive the wagons. When that happened, the moral climate was sometimes worse than it had been when the children walked to and from school.

9.51. *The Minnesota legislature convinced farmers to consolidate their schools by promising financial assistance for the building of new schoolhouses. The four one-room schools shown here were eliminated by the large consolidated school in the center. (U.S. Bureau of Education, Bulletin no. 5 [Washington, D.C.: GPO, 1911], pl. 8)*

9.53. Photographs showing large numbers of apparently happy schoolchildren poised for the ride home made consolidation appear as fortuitous as it was efficient. Center Consolidated School, Knox, Indiana. (Ind. State Library, Div. Picture Collection)

9.54. In the early 1900s, it was unreasonable to expect school wagons to be on time as they traveled over rural roads in winter and spring. Children in Wayne Township, Clinton County, Ohio, were transported over this road to reach their consolidated school. (OHS)

But there were more personal reasons for the farmers' reluctance to embrace consolidation. Like those in our own time, rural parents did not want their children transported from their neighborhood schools, where they had always been within reach. Fears of what might happen to them in the large distant school lurked in their minds. They worried that their children's clothes might not be good enough for the new school, that they might absorb the evils of the towns where most centralized schools were located, and that the town children would be unkind to them.

There were other fears as well. They knew, even if the reformers did not, that the loss of their schools meant the loss of their communities, around which their lives revolved. They were also unconvinced that new $12,000 schools could ever be less costly than their old one-roomers. But above all else, most midwestern farmers saw consolidation as just one more scheme by the educators to take the schools from their control, and they would not have it.

The result was that consolidation had barely dented the old school system in the Midwest—with the exception of Ohio and Indiana—by the end of World War I. Up and down that region, thousands of one-room schools—with dwindling enrollments and tight budgets, but still controlled by the farmers they served—lived on into the 1920s and 1930s, when the Great Depression helped dampen the enthusiasm for more consolidations.

Chapter

10

The Depression Years

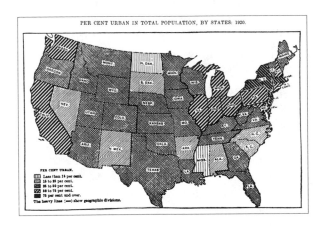

10.1. *In eight of the twelve midwestern states, more people still lived in rural areas in 1920.* (Fourteenth Census of the United States: Population, *vol. 1* [Washington, D.C.: GPO, 1921], p. 48)

On November, 11, 1918, World War I ended abruptly. Swollen wartime farm prices tumbled, and depression once more struck the farmland. In the hard times that followed, the rural renaissance no longer drew public attention. Like many revivals, it was short-lived. Still, new schoolhouses, improved roads, rural telephones, mail delivery, and a bundle of new farm legislation testified to its vigor in those golden years before the First World War.

But in spite of all this, the rural renaissance had not kept farm children on the farm. Through the early 1900s, rural Americans continued to flock to the cities as they had for years. In 1920, for the first time in the nation's history, the census showed more Americans living in towns and cities than in the country. [Table 10.1] And although eight of the twelve midwestern states had remained largely rural, one midwestern newspaper called the results of the new census a "thunderclap revealing a condition dreaded by sociologists and patriots." And so it was [Illus. 10.1]

The worst fears of those who had worried over the loss of the nation's farmers multiplied as they contemplated the future. Could the nation's

Table 10.1. Urban and Rural Population of the United States, 1790–1940

Census Year	% of Population	
	Urban	Rural
1940	56.5	43.5
1930	56.2	43.8
1920	51.2	48.8
1910	45.7	54.3
1900	39.7	60.3
1890	35.1	64.9
1880	28.2	71.8
1870	25.7	74.3
1860	19.8	80.2
1850	15.3	84.7
1840	10.8	89.2
1830	8.8	91.2
1820	7.2	92.8
1810	7.3	92.7
1800	6.1	93.9
1790	5.1	94.9

SOURCE: *Sixteenth Census of the United States: 1940. Population*, Vol. 1 (Washington, D.C.: GPO, 1942), p. 18.
The classification of urban or rural is based on 1940 definitions.

values and institutions—church, family, school, ideals, and even government—which had been shaped for three hundred years in a rural environment for a rural people withstand the corruption and decadence of cities? It was a question that had been asked before by American artists and intellectuals as they saw their nation retreat from the soil. But strangely, they seemed less anxious about cities than they had once been.

10.2. Assigned to illustrate rural poverty to help secure favorable farm legislation in the depression years, FSA photographers revealed the achievements of the rural renaissance in their photos of rural roads and mailboxes. This Iowa farmhouse along Highway 6 was photographed in February 1940. (LC)

The superintendent of the 1920 census—unlike his predecessor in 1890, who inspired a new interpretation of the nation's past by predicting the end of the nation's frontier—apparently perceived no great significance in the population shift of 1920. Neither did many scholars, in spite of the fears that urbanization had aroused in them in the past.

Perhaps their nonchalance can be explained by the fact that, despite the statistics, much of the nation remained rural between the two world wars. Country people who migrated to the cities both before and after World War I took their rural values with them, so for a time, at least, large portions of the cities remained rural at heart. In 1928, the country was still not ready for an urban president with a bowler hat and cigar.

Then, in the 1930s, the Great Depression cast its dark shadow across the land, slowing the trek to the cities more dramatically than the rural renaissance had ever done. Throughout that decade, scarcely three-tenths of 1 percent of the nation's rural people moved to cities. Not since the second decade of the nineteenth century had so few Americans left the farms for the cities (see Table 10.1). In addition, thousands of Americans with ties to the land—parents or grandparents still living on the old homestead—returned to the country, where they could raise their own food and avoid the charity they were too proud to accept. Illinois, Indiana, Michigan, and Ohio—the most urbanized midwestern states—all showed a loss of urban population between 1930 and 1940.

The fact that the nation remained basically rural in spirit if not in numbers was, perhaps, a major reason it survived the great economic calamity of the 1930s with its democratic institutions intact. In any case, rural values and rural democracy remained largely unshaken in the midwestern heartland. There, neither the steady rhythm of farm life nor the rural landscape had greatly changed from 1900 to the 1930s, when photographers tramped through the area taking pictures for the federal Farm Security Administration (FSA). Never before had the rural Midwest been so thoroughly photographed. As if they knew that this was their last chance to picture a vanishing America, these indefatigable photographers unmasked every wrinkle on the face of the land and captured for posterity not merely the appearance but the very feel of midwestern farm life. Setting out to paint the dark side of rural America to help secure favorable farm legislation, they succeeded mainly in portraying the changelessness of the midwestern farmland and the courage of its people in the face of the Great Depression. Of course, their cameras also recorded changes that the rural renaissance had brought to the midwestern countryside before World War I. Quiet country roads, improved for rural free delivery of mail and passable even in winter, showed up in dozens of photographs. So, too, did the rural mailboxes that stood on wintry days like friendly sentries before every farm gate. [Illus. 10.2] Along those same roads, stretching as far as the eye could see across snow-covered fields, were telephone poles—planted there in more optimistic years, when it was thought possible to keep farmers on the farm by ending their rural isolation. [Illus. 10.3]

In a single photograph, one photographer immortalized two emblems of the nearly forgotten rural uplift: a telephone pole and a school wagon used years earlier to transport children to consolidated schools where, presumably, they would receive a better education. [Illus. 10.4] Other photographers captured some of those fine consolidated schools, such as the four-teacher one at Bear Creek, Minnesota, which represented the educators' final solution to the problem of rural education. [Illus. 10.5]

Yet their cameras' searching eyes found more unchanged than changed. Their shutters opened and closed on a countryside that seemed almost to have stood still from the early 1900s on, while life in the cities hurried on around it. A Rip Van Winkle, roused from a sleep of forty years, would have seen few changes in the farm community near Carrolltown, Missouri, photographed in 1943. The farmhouse, barns, horses, and machinery in the picture's foreground, scattered farms, and a putative one-room school in the distance were surely as familiar to Americans of 1900 as they were to those of World War II. [Illus. 10.6]

Elsewhere, a solitary Nebraska farmhouse built years before—its windmill and outbuildings

10.3. Telephone lines—designed to break the farmers' isolation—stretched for miles along rural midwestern highways, much like this one in Grundy County, Iowa. (LC)

10.4. In this picture, an FSA photographer immortalized two emblems of the rural renaissance: a telephone pole and an abandoned wagon that was once used to carry children to consolidated schools. Williams County, North Dakota, October 1937. (LC)

10.5. *One reminder of the rural renaissance was this consolidated four-teacher schoolhouse at Bear Creek, Minnesota. (Minn. State Dept. of Education)*

10.7. *A solitary Nebraska farmhouse suggested the enduring loneliness of farm life in the age of the Great Depression, May 1939. (LC)*

beacon-like against a lowering spring sky—suggested the enduring isolation of farm life on the plains, even in the 1930s. [Illus. 10.7] Across the state line, the early 1900s lived on in a tidy Iowa farmhouse sitting on the brow of a hill overlooking a pasture, where white-faced cattle grazed on an early autumn day. [Illus. 10.8] A country road ran past it to meet another road, which, in turn, connected with still another to empty, finally—as so many did—in a small rural village that was as much a part of the rural panorama as the farms themselves. [Illus. 10.9] But nothing suggested the unchanging face of the rural Midwest more than a one-room schoolhouse sitting opposite a trim farmstead nestled among the Iowa hills. [Illus. 10.10]

The photographers found its counterparts along many country roads. This may have surprised them at first. With Model T's and Model A's everywhere, they might have supposed most one-room schools had disappeared. But they had not. Still active, still inextricably woven into the fabric of midwestern rural life, they marked the failure of the reformers' consolidation efforts as well as the conservatism of rural ways.

Nearly 70,000 one-room schoolhouses still checkered the midwestern landscape in 1936, which was more than half of all those remaining in the nation. Between them, Illinois and Iowa had more than 19,000, and each had more than any other state. [Table 10.2] Slightly more than 58 percent of all schoolhouses in the five states of the Old Northwest were one room; in the other

10.6. *A Rip Van Winkle, waking from a sleep of forty years, would have found this panorama of a midwestern farm community—with its scattered farms and one-room schoolhouse—little changed in 1943. Near Carrollton, Missouri, March 1943. (LC)*

10.8. *The early 1900s lived on in this Iowa farmstead set on the brow of a hill in Marshall County, Iowa, October 1939. (LC)*

Table 10.2. Midwestern One-Room Schoolhouses, 1935–1936

Region	Number	% of Total Schoolhouses Used
Continental U.S.	132,813	55.6
Illinois	9,925	71.1
Indiana	1,363	39.1
Iowa	9,115	77.0
Kansas	6,777	72.1
Michigan	5,124	62.0
Minnesota	6,797	79.4
Missouri	7,357	71.8
Nebraska	5,958	75.3
North Dakota	4,077	75.1
Ohio	2,451	39.8
South Dakota	4,441	88.5
Wisconsin	6,529	79.2
Total Midwest	69,914	

SOURCE: U.S. Office of Education, Bulletin, 1937, No. 2, Chap. 2., vol. 2 (Washington, D.C.: GPO, 1940), p. 79.

10.9. *Photographers pictured country roads passing midwestern farms to meet other roads that emptied into small towns, which were as much a part of the rural landscape as the farms themselves. Dickens, Iowa, December 1936. (LC)*

seven midwestern states, one-room schoolhouses were 77 percent of the total. So numerous were they that the photographers could not possibly have missed them. Nor, apparently, did they wish to. What better way to evoke the pathos of rural life in the depression years than a picture of a lonely one-room schoolhouse on the wind-swept prairie of North Dakota? [Illus. 10.11] Or how better to illustrate the barrenness of rural life and the lack of educational opportunities than a scene of two small boys in overalls, possibly the school's only children, lolling at recess in the grass near a weather-beaten privy? To help make his point, the photographer labeled the picture the "cut-over land" in Wisconsin. [Illus. 10.12]

In this collection of photographs, now in the Library of Congress, was seemingly certain proof that midwestern farm children were underprivileged. At the very least, the photographs documented how little the rural renaissance had altered the essentials of midwestern country school education, which had been in existence for over three-quarters of a century. Even in that auto age, children walked a mile or more to school on raw winter days, books in hand, along lonely country roads, just as their parents and grandparents had done before them. [Illus. 10.13]

True, parents and children were beginning to

pitch in to prepare hot lunches in one-room schools here and there in the 1920s and 1930s, but that was uncommon. [Illus. 10.14] Sometimes forsaking the lard bucket of yesteryear for a store-bought lunch pail, thousands of country children still carried their lunches to school. Following a noontime pattern that was generations old, they ate—weather permitting—at some chosen place on their unkempt school yard. [Illus. 10.15]

In the schools' cloakrooms, children of the depression hung their coats as country children had always done. Even their wraps—torn, threadbare, apparent hand-me-downs—were little dif-

10.10. *The durable institutions of the rural Midwest were reflected in still-active one-room schoolhouses like this one, across the road from a tidy Iowa farmstead in Monroe County in 1940. (LC)*

10.11. *Photographs of lonely one-room schoolhouses on windswept prairies evoke the pathos of rural life during the Great Depression. (LC)*

10.12. *A photographer saw rural poverty and blunted opportunities in this scene of farmers' children at recess at a one-room school in what he called the "cut-over land" in Wisconsin, in the vicinity of Tipler in May 1937. (LC)*

10.13. *Midwestern farm children still walked to and from school on raw windy days, much as their parents and grandparents had done in years gone by. Vicinity of Mobridge, South Dakota, February 1942. (LC)*

10.14. *Hot lunches donated by farm families and prepared by the children were served in some schools in the 1930s, as in this school in Walworth County, Wisconsin. (Whi [X3] 45954, SHSW)*

10.15. *For children of the depression, the noontime meal was a picnic in the corner of the school yard on warm days, as it had been for their predecessors. Here and there, however, store-bought lunch pails replaced the lard buckets used by earlier generations. Grundy County, Iowa, October 1937. (LC)*

ferent from those their predecessors had worn to school, even in better times. [Illus. 10.16]

Noon hours and recesses—those blessed respites in the school day—were consumed in activities that were familiar to anyone who had ever attended a country school. The hurried donning of coats and boots in the cloakroom, the rush to the playground, and the fox-and-geese circle in the snow were rural school rituals as old as the oldest country school. [Illus. 10.17–10.19] Only WPA-variety privies added a touch not seen in 1900.

Midwestern one-room schools did not survive into the age of the Great Depression because

10.16. *Depression-era children hung their torn and threadbare wraps in the same cloakrooms their parents had used years before. Williams County, North Dakota, October 1937. (LC)*

10.18. *Only their sparse numbers made this scene of children rushing to play different from that of a bygone era. Morton County, North Dakota, February 1942. (LC)*

10.17. *On winter days, children hurriedly donned coats, pants, and overshoes–if they had them–in preparation for outdoor play during the noon hour. Morton County, North Dakota, February 1942. (LC)*

10.19. *Playing fox-and-geese in the snow was a mid-western ritual as old as the oldest one-room school. Morton County, North Dakota, February 1942. (LC)*

educators had given up trying to change the system. In the 1920s and 1930s, they continued to argue for consolidation and gathered statistics to prove that one-room schools were too small to be efficient. Grundy County, Missouri, was cited as an example of how to save money and provide a better education. Almost unchanged since its beginning, Grundy County had seventy-eight separate school districts in the early 1930s, each with a separate administrative unit. All told, there were 83 schools and 252 school directors. [Illus. 10.20] Most of these were farmers who, with their neighbors, still levied their own school taxes and employed their own teachers. In the

county's seventy-five one-room schools, each teacher taught an average of only sixteen pupils.

A revised map of the county illustrated how the reformers thought a school system should look. They would reduce the seventy-eight small districts to five, build one school in each district, eliminate all the rest, and create only one school board for the entire county. [Illus. 10.21] But the farmers here, as elsewhere across the nation's middle section, remained as reluctant in the 1930s to give up their little schools as they had been during the rural renaissance.

Between 1926 and 1934, the number of con-

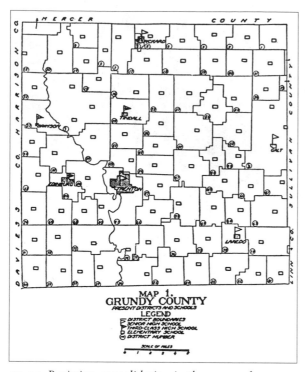

10.20. *Resisting consolidation in the 1930s, farmers in Grundy County, Missouri, maintained eighty-three schools and seventy-eight separate districts, with 252 school directors. (U.S. Office of Education, Bulletin no. 3 [Washington, D.C.: GPO, 1934], p. 38)*

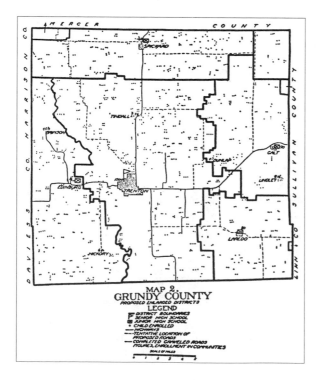

solidations nationwide had increased by 27 percent. By 1933–34, there were more than 17,000 consolidated schools in the continental United States. Most of these—almost 8,000—were in the South, where small, independent, self-governing school systems had never really taken root and where the educational system was less democratic than it was elsewhere. In the Midwest, however, where farmers had controlled their own schools for more than a century, there were scarcely more than 4,000 consolidated schools—some of them only two-room affairs—after more than thirty years of reform efforts (U.S. Office of Education, Bulletin no. 2 [Washington, D.C.: GPO, 1937], p. 70). Nebraska had only 71 consolidated schools in 1934 and more than 6,000 one-room schools. No wonder the photographer who caught the children at recess at the District No. 112 school in Seward County, Nebraska, noted that "Nebraska's school system was little consolidated." According to him, "these little white schools [were] on the county crossroads throughout the state." [Illus. 10.22]

If reason was on the side of educators, passion moved the farmers. "Tradition, sentiment, personal prejudice, and convenience," explained one educator, "stand in the way [of reform]." All this was true, and these attitudes, which perhaps only farmers could understand, apparently hardened in those years that the locusts were eating.

Actually, the depression did encourage some consolidations, as here and there little districts banded together. But on the whole, it was a poor time to try to convince midwestern farmers to give up their schools. The times were too hard to give much thought to school reform. Farm foreclosures were everywhere, and forced sales left once prosperous farmers with almost nothing. Driven from the farms they had owned, they became tenants on other farms or drifted from the land to join the ranks of the unemployed.

Left: 10.21. *Educational experts envisioned a reorganization of Grundy County, Missouri, reducing its seventy-eight districts with eighty-three schools to five districts with one school each. (U.S. Office of Education, Bulletin no. 3 [Washington, D.C.: GPO, 1934], p. 39)*

Table 10.3. Teachers' Salaries and Warrants, 1934

State	Teachers' Salaries in Arrears	Warrants Constituting an Emergency
Illinois	$28,000,000	$5,000,000
Michigan	1,000,000	2,000,000
Minnesota	—	2,350,000
Missouri	250,000	750,000
Nebraska	290,000	1,650,000
Ohio	16,525,000	3,125,000
South Dakota	—	2,500,000

SOURCE: *Congressional Record*, 73 Cong., 2d Sess. (June 9, 1934), pp. 10952–53.

10.22. *The FSA photographer who shot this one-room school in District No. 112, Seward County, Nebraska, found such little white schoolhouses at country crossroads throughout the state and commented that "the Nebraska school system was little consolidated" in October 1938. (LC)*

Even the weather conspired against them in the dust bowl; swirling winds piled sand dunes in their fields and school yards, where exuberant children ran over them at recesss. [Illus. 10.23]

In the midst of this crisis, farmers had trouble simply keeping their little schools open, to say nothing of building new consolidated schools. As the depression swept over the countryside, farm values dropped like a rock in a well, and so did taxes, which often could not be collected in any case. By the spring of 1934, a number of midwestern school districts were already millions of dollars in arrears in their tax collections, with no prospect of collecting them in the foreseeable future.

The bankruptcy of local government spread to country schools like an epidemic. Gone was the time when farmers could gather in their schoolhouses and confidently tax themselves to pay their teachers' salaries for a nine-month school term. Unlike the urban schools, they could not eliminate the educational frills, since they had so few. All they could do was reduce their teachers' salaries and shorten their school terms to seven, six, five, or even three months. But for some districts, even this was not enough, and a number of one-room schools that had withstood a century or more of troubles were forced to close their doors, at least temporarily. [Illus. 10.24]

For many other farmers, the specter of closing their schools haunted them. To ward off the evil day, many districts paid their teachers in warrants that were either not redeemable in cash or only partly so. By 1934, the salaries of teachers in five midwestern states were far in arrears, and school warrants amounting to millions in those

and other states were of doubtful value. [Table 10.3] Some teachers did, in fact, teach for nothing for a time.

Only the timely help of federal funds kept many of the region's one-room schools open. Funneled through the Civil Works Administration and the Federal Emergency Relief Administration (FERA), the money was used to pay teachers' salaries through 1933 and 1934. In the

10.23. *In the Midwest's dust bowl, children played on sand dunes piled high in the school yard. (SHSI, Iowa City)*

Table 10.4. *Funds Allotted by FERA for Rural School Continuation in the Midwest, 1933–1934*

State	November	December	June
Illinois	—	$73,600	$73,600
Indiana	—	49,500	49,500
Iowa	—	6,200	35,500
Kansas	—	7,000	7,000
Michigan	—	50,000	50,000
Minnesota	—	15,000	37,000
Missouri	$7,500	51,000	51,000
Nebraska	—	18,500	18,500
North Dakota	—	8,500	8,500
Ohio	—	65,000	110,000
South Dakota	800	7,000	11,500
Wisconsin	9,356	41,821	41,821

SOURCE: U.S. Congress, House of Representatives, 73 Cong., 2d Sess., Feb. 26–Mar. 1, 1934 (Washington, D.C.: GPO, 1934), pp. 36–37.

FAIRVIEW NEWS

Fairview School opened Monday, Sept. 3rd with nineteen pupils enrolled. Miss Marion Earl who has taught two years previously has been re-engaged as teacher of the school.

The annual chicken fry held at Fairview for patrons and friends of the school will be held Friday night, September 14.

Decide what you want and then go after it.

Monday was one of those days the gloom chaser should have been busy.

It would be interesting to find out what the people are doing who six months ago were spending most of their time worrying about inflation.

10.25. Midwestern farmers may have found some comfort in the county weekly's simple announcement that school had opened in the fall as it always had. (Argenta, Ill., Register, Sept. 7, 1934, p. 3)

spring of 1935, while Congress debated the wisdom and constitutionality of such federal aid to education, hundreds of little midwestern country schools were, in effect, still on relief. [Table 10.4]

Now more than ever, the farmers had reason to fear the loss of control of their schools and the taxes that might be levied to support consolidation. But resistance to consolidation sprang from other sources as well. With so many farmers losing their farms and moving to cities or rented places, the small school down the road was one of the few constants in the lives of those who

remained in the community. Perhaps they even found some comfort and reassurance when they read the county weekly's simple announcement that the school had opened as usual. [Illus. 10.25]

The very existence of the one-room schools meant the continuation of their communities. Country schoolhouses had always been the center of the midwestern farmers' social lives, and in the days of trouble the schools provided an even more important setting for the entertainment that helped make the farmers' depression-filled lives bearable. Even when automobiles made it possible for them to travel far from their farms, they still gathered at the schoolhouse for programs, picnics, PTA and community club meetings, and simple get-togethers. The county weeklies were filled with descriptions of social events held at the schoolhouse, revealing just how midwestern farm families were able to enjoy life during the worst economic crisis they had ever endured. If they had little else, they had the satisfaction of seeing their children being educated in the face of adversity and the joy of gathering at the little schoolhouse and sharing bountiful meals with friends and neighbors. [Illus. 10.26]

In addition, between New Deal programs and the onset of World War II, the one-room schoolhouses were needed for more kinds of meetings than the farmers would ever have imagined. Farm Bureau, rural electrification, soil conservation, and Food for Victory meetings were only some of the new uses the farmers found for their schoolhouses during the depression. [Illus. 10.27]

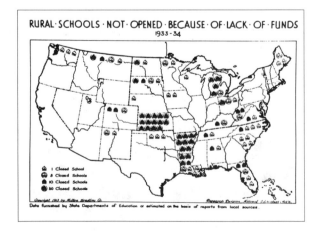

10.24. More than two hundred midwestern one-room schools were among the hundreds nationwide that were unable to open in 1933 and 1934 because of the Great Depression. (U.S. Office of Education, Leaflet no. 44 [Washington, D.C.: GPO, 1934])

Grand Picnic

More than three hundred of the best citizens of this community gathered at the Brown schoolhouse Sunday for a regular good old time picnic. If everyone present did not have a good time it was nobody's fault but their own, as everyone apparently came with but one idea in view and that was to have a good sociable time. Cars began to roll in about eleven o'clock and unload baskets and in a short time, two tables 50 feet long were filled with all the good eats you could think of. To look at those tables you would not think there were any hard times around here. While the ladies prepared dinner, men played horseshoes and softball to work up an appetite and they were sure ready to do justice to the fine dinner. After the dinner an excellent program was put on by old and young. After the election of officers for next year a very happy day had passed. The following were elected:

Pres.—Charles Hilbrant
V. Pres.—Russell McGiunis
Sec't'y.—Mrs. Minnie Parr
Treas.—Mrs. O. S. Turner

Next year the picnic will be at the Brown school house on the last Sunday of July. The President invites you to invite your friends and make this a real community picnic, and have one day to forget our troubles and have a good time.

Plenty of room, lots of shade, abundance of water, an ideal place for a picnic.

10.27. Midwestern farmers gathered at their schoolhouses for meetings of all kinds, including this Food for Victory meeting in Adams County, North Dakota, February 1942. (LC)

dred old schoolhouses were moved from their sites and replaced with modern schools like those designed during the rural renaissance. [Illus. 10.30] Where new schoolhouses could not be built, touches were added to the old ones in many districts to make the classrooms more comfortable and the grounds more enjoyable for the children. Swings, merry-go-rounds, and turning bars—once nonexistent on most country school yards—appeared on the school grounds in all but the very poorest of districts in the 1920s and 1930s. [Illus. 10.31]

Flags and flagpoles were also prominent features in almost every country school yard. Patri-

So the farmers clung to their one-room schools, many of which had been built in the preceding century or the early 1900s. Many had, of necessity, been left unpainted and uncared for in the hard times of the 1930s. [Illus. 10.28] In 1935, a survey of 8,217 one-room schools in Kansas revealed that 3,949 were more than thirty-five years old, and some had scarcely changed over the years. Of the total, 7,168 had no slides for the playgrounds; 832 had no recreational equipment at all; and, like others all over the Midwest, 1,355 still had no wells (Kansas State Planning Board, *Rural Schools in Kansas, March 1935: A Study of Their Physical Condition and Recreational Equipment* [n.p., n.d.]). In such schools, water was supplied by older boys, who ferried it from a nearby farm in a routine as old as the log schoolhouse. [Illus. 10.29]

Yet even during hard times, new one-room schools continued to be built here and there throughout the region in the 1920s and on into the depression years. In Sioux County, Iowa, between 1918 and the 1940s, more than a hun-

10.28. During the Great Depression, many midwestern one-room schoolhouses like this one in District No. 1, Logan County, Kansas, were left unpainted and unrepaired. Compare this picture with Illus. 4.19 to see the depression's toll. (KSHS)

10.29. *In the age of the Great Depression, schoolboys continued to supply water from nearby farms for the hundeds of one-room schools that were still without wells. Arrow Lodge School, Walworth County, Wisconsin. (Whi [X3] 45955, SHSW)*

10.30. *In spite of the depression, old schoolhouses in Sioux County, Iowa, and elsewhere were uplifted and moved between 1918 and 1940 to make way for new schools of the kind built during the rural renaissance. (SHSI, Iowa City)*

otism, as opposed to other "isms" of the time, generally remained firm in the countryside, even during the Great Depression. Scarcely a school was now without its ritual of having the children line up to salute the flag and repeat the Pledge of Allegiance. [Illus. 10.32]

By the end of the decade, thanks to rural electrification, electricity had replaced the old kerosene lamps in some of the humblest and oldest of schoolhouses. [Illus. 10.33] Another improvement that occurred during the depression was the increased attention paid to school sanitation. New outdoor privies were built by the Works Progress Administration (WPA), and some states provided for the inspection of country schools to make certain that they were as clean as possible. [Illus. 10.34] In older days, hardly anyone would have noticed whether the floor was treated for dust or whether the school's water supply was being polluted by nearby privies. [Illus. 10.35]

Country children also benefited from improved libraries and from other changes that took place inside schoolrooms in the 1920s and 1930s. In old one-room buildings, nothing could be done about the chimney at one end of the room or the stovepipe running the length of the ceiling, but stoves were improved. Victrolas, and even radios, became almost commonplace in one-room schoolrooms. Movable, self-contained

10.31. *Between the two worlds wars, swings, merry-go-rounds, and other playground equipment became common in midwestern country school yards, where once only the children's imaginations had provided their games. Starke County, North Dakota, 1942. (LC)*

desks replaced those nailed-to-the-floor affairs that generations of country children had used. [Illus. 10.36]

There were differences, too, in the education of country children. One was the switch in readers inadvertently registered by an FSA photographer in a North Dakota school. [Illus. 10.37] For better or worse, the *Dick and Jane* series replaced the old moralistic *McGuffey's Readers*, whose poems and orations so many midwestern schoolchildren had memorized and cherished. This change may have harmonized with the new goals for rural education. Eschewing the three Rs, these goals, according to one educator, were:

1. To learn how to get along with other people.

2. To protect and maintain one's health.

3. To learn wise uses of leisure time.

4. To develop the skills and understanding needed to solve the problems of one's home, community, and individual life.

During the Great Depression, educators gave much thought to improving rural teaching and even created what was called a "differentiated curriculum" for country teachers. It was composed principally of courses such as country school curriculum, administration, management,

10.33. Rural electrification allowed the substitution of electric lights for kerosene lamps in even the oldest one-room schoolhouses. West Branch School, Wisconsin. (LC)

10.32. In the age of the Great Depression, scarcely any one-room school was without a flag and flagpole and the Pledge of Allegiance ceremony. (SHSI, Des Moines)

COUNTY HEALTH DEPARTMENT
Rural School Sanitation Report

School Poorman   Township Pennfield

Director O. J. Dunlap   Teacher Lucille Walker

SITE:
☑ Ample area
☑ Well drained and graded
☑ Grounds clean
☑ Play equipment Swings & Teeter
☐ Adequate

BUILDING:
☑ Good repair
☑ Building screened
☐ Fire extinguisher

WATER SUPPLY:
☑ Good location
☑ Proper construction
☐ Safe analysis
☑ Accessibility
☑ Suitable container
☑ Sanitary fountain or sanitary cups
☐ Proper transportation

TOILETS:
☑ Good location
☑ Proper construction
☑ Proper maintenance

VENTILATION:
☑ Sufficient circulation of air
☑ Window ventilators
☑ Windows adjustable, top and bottom
☑ = Satisfactory
× = Improvement needed

HEATING: Basement
☑ Circulating furnace or jacketed stove
☑ Water pan (Humidity _____
☐ Thermometer (_____° F.)

LIGHTING:
☑ Absence of glare
☑ Sufficient light
  Natural (sill 300 f.c.) (desk 3 f.c.
  Artificial (desk 9 f.c.)
☑ Tan translucent shades
☒ Walls properly decorated Green ceili
☑ Shades up, curtains back
☑ Position of shade rollers

ROOM CLEANLINESS:
☒ Floors treated for dust
☑ Floor and furniture clean
☑ Windows and light fixtures clean
☒ Condition of blackboards Composition
☐ Proper refuse disposal

PERSONAL HYGIENE:
☑ Individual or paper towels
☑ Powdered or liquid soap
☑ Proper washing facilities
☐ First aid material

SEATING:
☒ Proper seats
☒ Spacing of seats

Improvements since last inspection Electricity

Remarks: 1. Ceiling and walls decorated in cream or flat white and natural lighting. 2. Slate blackboards are easier on pupils eyes.
3. Adjustable seating equipment is recommended.
Date May 18, 1937   Inspected by SHP

10.34. Midwestern one-room schools were made more sanitary and hence healthier by regular inspections in some states in the 1930s. This report was for the Poorman School in District No. 1, Pennfield Township, Calhoun County, Michigan. (School Records, Mich. Historical Collections, Bentley Historical Library, Univ. of Mich.)

10.35. *Concern for the proximity of the boys' toilet to the water supply led school authorities to examine this school in District No. 95, Hennepin County, Minnesota. (Minn. State Dept. of Education)*

10.36. *Even in the depression years, improved libraries, new stoves, Victrolas, and movable self-contained desks enhanced one-room classrooms across the Midwest. Top: Country school library in Wright County, Minnesota. (MHS) Bottom: Classroom, Eagle Corners, Wisconsin (Whi [X3] 1335, SHSW)*

methods, and practice teaching. Of 184 normal schools surveyed in 1937, 73 percent gave such courses, and only 29 percent gave courses in subject matter. [Table 10.5]

The value of such courses may have been lost on country teachers, who had to teach the eight common branches plus agriculture to children in grades one through eight. In any case, their exposure to this curriculum was probably not extensive. Only 38 percent of teachers in one- and two-room schools nationwide had two years or more of college in the late 1930s. Perhaps this explained why country teachers continued to teach much as they always had. Aside from the smaller student body and changes in feminine dress, the country classroom photographed in Grundy County, Iowa, in 1939 might easily have been taken for a schoolroom in the 1890s. The torn window shade, the history lesson on the board, and the children studying at desks that were pegged to the floor and arranged according to their ages suggested how little things had changed since these children's parents and grandparents had attended the same school years before. Perhaps the teacher at the blackboard helping her second-grade pupil with his arithmetic was the most noticeable difference from the past, when the teacher would probably have had more than one second-grade student. [Illus. 10.38]

This scene was reenacted daily in hundreds of schoolrooms across the Midwest in the depression years. In the mid-1930s, except for those in Illinois, Indiana, Michigan, and Ohio, nearly a quarter of all midwestern children were still being educated in one-room schools. [Table 10.6] In these schools, the rituals of schooling harked back to the 1890s and beyond. In all of the Midwest, scarcely a county weekly was published that did not include notices of box suppers, programs, Christmas plays, and picnics on the last glorious day of school, all to be held at the one-room schoolhouse. [Illus. 10.39] The county weeklies also continued to make much of the eighth-grade graduations, when graduates of one-room schools from every corner of the

Table 10.5. Courses Offered for Preparation of Country Schoolteachers in 184 Normal Schools, 1936

	No. of Institutions	% of Institutions
Professional courses	134	73
Rural school practice teaching	92	50
Rural school observation	67	36
Rural school administration	48	26
Rural school management	93	51
Rural school curriculum	48	26
Rural school methods	47	26
Rural school libraries	4	2
Rural school seminar or surveys	12	7
Background courses	109	59
Rural community activities and relations	34	19
Rural sociology	94	51
Rural economics	28	15
Differentiated subject-matter courses	53	29
Reading and English	17	9
Mathematics	8	4
Agriculture and nature study	19	10
Elementary science	3	2
Geography	9	5
Social sciences	6	3
Health and physical education	17	9
Home economics	12	7
Industrial arts	12	7
Music	18	10
Fine arts	11	6
Handwriting	1	0.5

SOURCE: U.S. Office of Education, Bulletin, 1937, No. 2, Chap. 5, Vol. 1 (Washington, D.C.: GPO, 1940), p. 29.

Table 10.6. Midwestern One-Room-School Enrollment, 1934–1935

State	Number of students	% of students
Illinois	169,726	12.8
Indiana	36,449	5.3
Iowa	140,536	26.1
Kansas	89,949	21.7
Michigan	123,610	12.8
Minnesota	141,012	25.7
Missouri	158,764	22.3
Nebraska	79,237	25.7
North Dakota	57,043	36.8
Ohio	57,502	4.5
South Dakota	63,791	41.6
Wisconsin	124,792	21.6

SOURCE: U.S. Office of Education, Pamphlet 92 (Washington, D.C.: GPO, 1940), p. 15.

county gathered at the county seat or nearby town to receive their diplomas. There they participated in a school program for the last time and were mentioned by name for their achievements. Nowhere else in all the nation was it possible to recognize the graduating eighth graders, as well as their parents, by name. [Illus. 10.40]

Were they underprivileged, these rural midwestern children of the Great Depression? In some ways, they were. In their makeshift clothes and worn, battered shoes, many were the poorest of the poor, and so were their schools. [Illus. 10.41] On the one hand, most could have profited—especially in the upper grades—from

10.37. *For better or worse, one-room schools forsook* McGuffey's Readers *for* Dick and Jane *during the Great Depression. Marshall County, North Dakota.* (LC)

10.38. *Advanced teacher training in the 1930s scarcely changed the day-to-day scenes in one-room classrooms such as this one in Grundy County, Iowa.* (LC)

Table 10.7. Occupations of Fathers of 12,715 Students in Nine Teachers' Colleges and Eight Liberal Arts Colleges in the North Central Association, 1930

Fathers' Occupation	Teachers' College Students		Liberal Arts Students		All Students	
	No.	%	No.	%	No.	%
Proprietary	1,143	13.7	879	20.1	2,022	15.9
Professional	922	11.9	967	22.1	1,959	15.4
Managerial	689	8.2	478	10.9	1,167	9.2
Commercial	652	7.8	424	9.7	1,076	8.5
Clerical	228	2.7	210	4.8	438	3.4
Agricultural	2,633	31.6	572	13.1	3,205	25.2
Building	401	4.8	146	3.4	547	4.3
Machine	414	5.0	200	4.6	614	4.8
Printing	44	0.5	43	0.9	87	0.6
Miscellaneous	183	2.2	88	2.0	271	2.2
Transportation-Communication	413	5.0	173	3.9	586	4.6
Protective	91	1.1	37	0.9	128	1.1
Personal	152	1.8	60	1.4	212	1.7
Extractive	91	1.1	16	0.4	107	0.8
Common	217	2.6	79	1.8	296	2.3

SOURCE: U.S. Office of Education, 1933, Bulletin No. 10, Chap. 1, Part 2 (Washington, D.C.: GPO, 1935), p. 135.

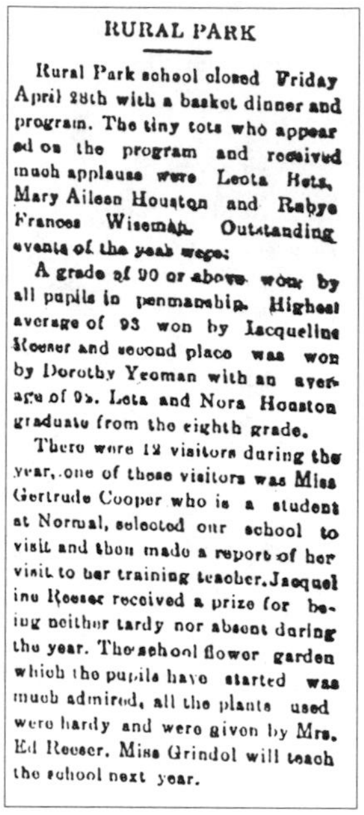

Table 10.8. Percentage of Persons Aged 25 Years and Older Completing Less Than Five Years of School, 1940

Division	%	Midwest State	%
Continental U.S.	13.5	Illinois	9.6
New England	10.1	Indiana	7.7
Middle Atlantic	12.2	Iowa	4.1
East North Central	9.1	Kansas	6.1
West North Central	7.5	Michigan	10.2
South Atlantic	22.9	Minnesota	7.5
East South Central	24.8	Missouri	10.3
West South Central	21.5	Nebraska	6.0
Mountain	11.0	North Dakota	10.8
Pacific	7.4	Ohio	8.4
		South Dakota	7.2
		Wisconsin	9.4

SOURCE: *Sixteenth Census of the United States: 1940*, Vol. 2 (Washington, D.C.: GPO, 1943), p. 84.

RURAL PARK

Rural Park school closed Friday April 28th with a basket dinner and program. The tiny tots who appeared on the program and received much applause were Leota Hetz, Mary Aileen Houston and Rubye Frances Wiseman. Outstanding events of the year were:

A grade of 90 or above won by all pupils in penmanship. Highest average of 93 won by Jacqueline Keener and second place was won by Dorothy Yeoman with an average of 9½. Leta and Nora Houston graduate from the eighth grade.

There were 12 visitors during the year, one of these visitors was Miss Gertrude Cooper who is a student at Normal, selected our school to visit and then made a report of her visit to her training teacher. Jacqueline Keener received a prize for being neither tardy nor absent during the year. The school flower garden which the pupils have started was much admired, all the plants used were hardy and were given by Mrs. Ed Reeser. Miss Grindol will teach the school next year.

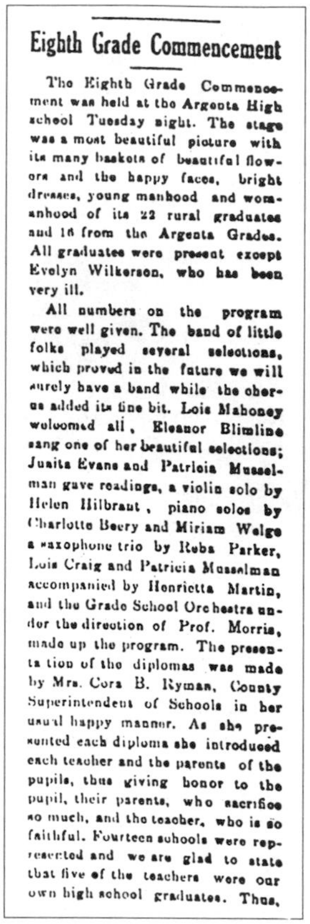

Eighth Grade Commencement

The Eighth Grade Commencement was held at the Argenta High school Tuesday night. The stage was a most beautiful picture with its many baskets of beautiful flowers and the happy faces, bright dresses, young manhood and womanhood of its 22 rural graduates and 16 from the Argenta Grades. All graduates were present except Evelyn Wilkerson, who has been very ill.

All numbers on the program were well given. The band of little folks played several selections, which proved in the future we will surely have a band while the others added its fine bit. Lois Mahoney welcomed all, Eleanor Blimline sang one of her beautiful selections; Juanita Evans and Patricia Musselman gave readings, a violin solo by Helen Hilbrant, piano solos by Charlotte Beery and Miriam Weigs a saxophone trio by Reba Parker, Lois Craig and Patricia Musselman accompanied by Henrietta Martin, and the Grade School Orchestra under the direction of Prof. Morris, made up the program. The presentation of the diplomas was made by Mrs. Cora B. Ryman, County Superintendent of Schools in her usual happy manner. As she presented each diploma she introduced each teacher and the parents of the pupils, thus giving honor to the pupil, their parents, who sacrifice so much, and the teacher, who is so faithful. Fourteen schools were represented and we are glad to state that five of the teachers were our own high school graduates. Thus,

Left: 10.39. The rituals of midwestern one-room schools, including picnics and programs on the last day of school, continued to be reported in county newspapers throughout the Great Depression. (Argenta, Ill., Register, May 5, 1933, p. 4)
Right: 10.40. In the rural Midwest, it was still possible during the Great Depression to publicly recognize country school graduates and their parents by name and to honor the best students. (Argenta, Ill., Register, May 25, 1933, p. 1)

larger libraries and some of the sophisticated teaching aids that were available in urban schools. On the other hand, children in the country schools had what money could not buy. They had small schools in which everyone was important and no one's identity was lost. They had stable families and parents who were interested in their education and especially in the school, which was peculiarly their own. Finally, unlike urban children, they had meaningful chores to do and the great outdoors, with its abundant resources for "learning by doing," which was the educational fad in the years between the two world wars. [Illus. 10.42] Whatever their advantages or disadvantages, thousands of graduates of midwestern one-room schools went on to high schools, colleges, and universities and eventually formed a large part of the nation's professional class.

To a generation with abundant opportunities to receive a higher education, it may seem odd that so many with so little ever went beyond the

Table 10.9. Midwestern One-Room Schoolhouses,
1941–1942

Region	Number of One-Room Schools	% of Teachers in One-Room Schools
Continental U.S	107,692	
Illinois	8,927	19.9
Indiana	871	4.1
Iowa	8,182	36.6
Kansas	5,894	35.7
Michigan	5,261	16.2
Minnesota	6,008	29.4
Missouri	6,504	26.4
Nebraska	5,495	41.0
North Dakota	3,280	43.3
Ohio	732	1.8
South Dakota	3,787	49.4
Wisconsin	5,408	26.9
Total Midwest	60,349	

SOURCE: U.S. Office of Education, *Biennial Survey of Education in the United States, 1941–1942* (Washington, D.C.: GPO, 1944), pp. 76–77.

10.42. Midwestern rural children lived in natural, largely unaltered surroundings and learned responsibility from their daily routine of chores. Crooked Creek School, Brown County, Indiana. (Ind. Univ. Foundation)

eighth grade. Yet a 1933 survey revealed that the largest percentage of students enrolled in nine teachers' colleges and eight liberal arts colleges in the North Central Association were children of farmers. [Table 10.7]

Even among those who did not go beyond grade school, there was no crisis of illiteracy. Few graduates of midwestern one-room schools could neither read nor write, and few had to be rejected for service in the army during World War II because of educational deficiencies. In 1940, the census no longer provided figures on the percentage of the population deemed illiterate. Instead, it gave the percentage of those who had less than a fifth-grade education—those whom the army considered to be illiterate. Once again, the Midwest had one of the lowest illiteracy rates. [Table 10.8]

By the time the nation entered World War II, some 107,000 one-room schools nationwide had weathered the troubles of the depression. Of these, more than 60,000 were in the twelve states of the Midwest. Illinois and Iowa, with over 17,000 combined, still led all the states in the number of such schools. [Table 10.9] Yet the end of these little schools was not far distant. When World War II was over, the farmers would no longer be able to resist efforts to eliminate their one-room schools, as they had done so often in the past.

10.41. Country children of the depression—were they underprivileged? Edell Roberts School, Brown County, Indiana. (Ind. Univ. Foundation)

Chapter

11

Consolidation at Last!

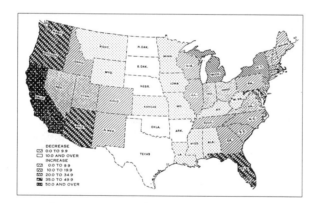

11.1. *Between 1940 and 1950, the loss of rural population in seven midwestern states was upwards of 9 percent. Only in the states of the Old Northwest was there any increase in the rural population.* (Report of the Seventeenth Decennial Census of the United States, *vol. 1 [Washington, D.C.: GPO., 1952], p. 23)*

World War II changed the rural Midwest no less than it did the rest of the nation. Ripping through the area like some great tornado, it uprooted families from ancestral farms, tossed them about in ever-widening circles, and set them down in towns and cities where they stayed, never to return to the land. Between 1940 and 1950, rural America lost over 3 percent of its people, but the loss in seven states of the Midwest ran upwards of 9 percent. Only in the states of the Old Northwest, where a majority of the population was already urban, was there any increase at all in the number of people living in rural areas. [Illus. 11.1]

Abandoned, desolate farmhouses that had once withstood the buffeting of children, spring planting, harvest, and cycles of boom and bust confirmed the statistics better than maps or graphs. [Illus. 11.2] So did the declining enrollments in the region's one-room schools. Near the close of World War II, the Midwest had more than 54,000 of the nation's 96,000 one-room schoolhouses still in use. [Table 11.1] But hundreds of these had fewer than ten pupils, and many had no more than five. Some had no pupils at all but were being maintained with the apparent expectation that one day there would be students for them.

The smallness of the schools, the improved black-topped highways, and buses that could speed children to distant schools combined to accomplish what the educators' arguments had been unable to do for so long. They so weakened the farmers' resistance to consolidation that the legislatures of every midwestern state (except for Ohio and Indiana, where consolidation was already far advanced) found the courage to pass laws providing for a revolutionary reorganization of school districts and the elimination of one-room schools. [Illus. 11.3]

Everywhere the laws were much the same. First, they established state boards to set standards and oversee the transformation from small to large school districts. Then they provided for county committees of laypeople to draw the actual plans for the redistricting of their counties. The final step, in recognition of the fact that democracy had always been at the heart of things in the Midwest, was a referendum to approve or reject the proposed reorganization. [Illus. 11.4]

Some states began this task less than a year after the end of the war; others started much later. In either case, it proved to be a mammoth and often unwelcome undertaking. Committees of laypeople, usually composed of a number of farmers, were forced to destroy the small schools they had defended and establish the consolida-

Table 11.1. Number of Midwestern One-Room Schoolhouses, 1931–1932 to 1953–1954

	1931–32	1943–44	1949–50	1953–54
United States	143,390	96,301	59,652	42,825
North Central	74,153	54,418	34,349	27,423
Illinois	10,041	8,361	2,370	722
Indiana	1,830	636	375	150
Iowa	9,279	7,563	4,173	3,594
Kansas	6,983	5,280	2,696	1,934
Michigan	6,141	3,791	2,707	2,538
Minnesota	6,888	5,409	3,948	2,831
Missouri	7,296	5,782	3,788	2,694
Nebraska	6,136	5,161	4,289	3,789
North Dakota	4,754	3,141	2,641	2,447
Ohio	3,747	640	341	200
South Dakota	4,731	3,599	3,065	2,775
Wisconsin	6,600	5,055	3,956	3,699

SOURCE: U.S. Office of Education. *Biennial Survey of Education in the United States, 1952–1954* (Washington, D.C.: GPO, 1959), Chap. 2, p. 38.

tions they had dreaded—almost as if in retribution for their long resistance to change. Boundary lines of the tiny school districts, many of them predating the Civil War, had to be erased. The new ones that were drawn dovetailed across the county and, in some cases, even across county borders.

Gigantically disruptive, the reconstruction was also an education for farmers and a showcase for grassroots democracy. Committee members who did not really believe in consolidation had to be educated about its necessity and then motivated to persuade independent-minded

11.2. *Desolate, abandoned farmhouses standing beside midwestern country roads, such as this one near Ellis Corners, Michigan, confirmed the loss of rural population revealed by the statistics.*

11.3. *New asphalt country roads like this one running past the old schoolhouse in District No. 2, Elba Township, Dodge County, Wisconsin, made it possible to bus country children to distant schools and weakened the farmers' resistance to consolidation.*

11.4. In the aftermath of World War II, midwestern state legislatures enacted laws establishing democratic procedures for consolidating the region's one-room schools, which led to their gradual disappearance. (Natoma, Kans., Independent, *Aug. 8, 1946, p. 5)*

SCHOOL DISTRICT
REORGANIZATION
PUBLICATION OF FINAL ORDER
THE STATE OF KANSAS to all interested parties and school patrons of common School Districts numbered 71-78-89-104-115 in Osborne County, Kansas:

You and each of you are hereby notified that the Osborne County School District Reorganization Committee has heretofore prepared plans for the reorganization of the territory contained in the above numbered school districts and has held public hearings upon such plans as required by Chapter 291, Session Laws of 1945 of the State of Kansas, and has reconsidered such plans in the light of the results of such hearings, and has now prepared and is publishing this FINAL ORDER of Reorganization as affecting the boundaries and reorganization of the Common School Districts above described.

You are also hereby notified that any interested party as defined by law who is dissatisfied with this order of the County Reorganization Committee may within 30 days from the date of the last publication of this order file an application with the Committee for a rehearing. Should no such application be filed within the time named, this order becomes final and will become fully effective on March 1, 1947.

Dated at Osborne, Kansas on this 23rd day of July, 1946.

The Osborne County School Reorganization Committee.

By:
J. E. Kissell, Chairman.
Geo. H. Nagel
Otto Fritsche
James Worley
Members of the Osborne County School Reorganization Committee.
ATTEST:
LaVerne Arnold
Secretary of the Osborne County School Reorganization Committee.

11.6. In 1946, when a photographer from Life *magazine shot this Illinois one-room school, the state still had thousands of such schools, but nearly all had diminished enrollments. (Bernard Hoffman,* Life, *Oct. 28, 1946, p. 91)*

11.5. Complaints against the consolidation of country schools were numerous. Some surfaced in the columns devoted to the social goings-on of rural communities. (Natoma, Kans., Independent, *June 6, 1946, p. 3)*

VICTOR

(This week's items)
What does your rural school mean to you? Is it worth fighting for or have you already been swallowed up by the "Big Five?" There has been a definite misuse of this School Reorganization law. This was designed merely to get rid of schools which had ceased to function. Not to come out here and sweep them clean as they come. No matter how hard we fought against it. If you want democracy to win, be at the Court House at Osborne Friday night, June 7 at 8 o'clock. Let's get behind District 6, in so doing, help our selves.

Mr. and Mrs. Paul Bricker and children spent Sunday evening at the Jean Bricker home.

Mr. and Mrs. Frank Mrawiec and Larry of Natoma came out to Victor church services Sunday evening.

Mr. and Mrs. Dan Goed, Mr. and Mrs. Dennis McNeal and L E. Murphy accompanied Mr. and Mrs. Eldon Winder to Osborne Friday evening to listen to the hearing of School District No. 6.

Mr. and Mrs Richard Sigle went to Hays Wednesday to attend the graduation exercises at Fort Hays State College. Richard was one of the graduates.

Mr. and Mrs. Ralph Murphy and boys ate supper Sunday evening with Mr. and Mrs. Eldon Winder and family.

Mr. and Mrs. Harye Case spent Sunday with Mr. and Mrs. Laurin Ewing.

farmers that reorganization was in their best interest. In state after state in those postwar years, reorganization was debated across every county and in every country schoolhouse. While local newspapers ran stories of the plans, the committees organized meetings and held public hearings to explain the proposals. The purpose was to give everyone a chance to express an opinion, which often became a protest against tearing up the old for something new and untried. [Illus. 11.5]

Whether because distances were shorter, roads better, country children fewer, or for some other reason, consolidation moved rapidly ahead in Illinois following the Reorganization Act of 1945. Just the year before, Illinois had had more than 8,000 one-room schoolhouses, and in 1946, thousands of them could still be found in every part of the state (see Table 11.1). In the autumn of that year, a photographer from *Life* magazine photographed a day in the life of one of them, District No. 95 in Winnebago County. Nostalgic and endearing to those who had once attended one-room schools, the familiar scenes were less so to critics, who saw in them the ills they had complained of since before the turn of the century.

It was, first of all, a small school. The teacher and fourteen children—the entire student body save one—stood in front of their schoolhouse for a group picture, as others had done for more than

11.7. *In District No. 95 in Winnebago County, Illinois, the activities of this one-room school photographed in 1946 had changed little from those of a generation before. Children played in the spacious school yard and, with unambiguous patriotism, began the school day with the Pledge of Allegiance. (Bernard Hoffman, Life, Oct. 28, 1946, pp. 93–94)*

11.8. *As in days gone by, the teacher in District No. 95, Winnebago County, Illinois, found work for all her students. She sent the second graders to the board, set the first grade to coloring, gave the seventh graders (on the far left) a problem to work, and held a recitation in geography with the sixth grade. (Bernard Hoffman, Life, Oct. 28, 1946, p. 92)*

three-quarters of a century. [Illus. 11.6] The photographer captured the children playing in the spacious school yard near those inconvenient and often unsanitary privies, where generations of children had played. He watched them enter their classroom and begin the day in the traditional rural way, with the Pledge of Allegiance to the flag. [Illus. 11.7] The teacher, who had taught at this school for twenty-six years, adhered to the schedule educators had found so inefficient. Following the Pledge of Allegiance, she sent the second graders to the board to do arithmetic problems, put others to work coloring or solving problems, and took up geography with the sixth grade. [Illus. 11.8]

These photographs were almost an epitaph for the one-room schools in Illinois. So swift was the consolidation after 1946 that by 1954, such schools were comparatively rare. In that year, fewer than 800 remained of the 10,000 existing in 1932 (see Table 11.1).

Though less dramatic than in Illinois, the reorganization in Kansas moved swiftly between 1945 and 1950. In those five years, almost half the state's one-room schools were eliminated (see Table 11.1). But there and elsewhere across the Midwest, after the first flurry of activity, consolidation inched forward school by school. As if they had suddenly confronted the magnitude of the changes taking place, farmers renewed their

Table 11.2. *One-Room Schools Nationwide, 1958*

Number of Schools	States
1–9	R.I., N.J., Conn.
10–20	Utah
21–29	Del., Md., S.C.
30–39	Ohio, La.
40–49	Mass., Fla., Ariz., Nev., Wash.
50–59	N.H.
60–69	Ga., N.C.
70–79	Idaho
80–89	Ind., N.Mex.
90–99	N.Y., Oreg.
100–199	Vt., Ark., Tex.
200–299	Maine, Ala., Colo., Wyo.
300–399	Va., Calif.
400–499	Pa., Ill., Miss., Okla.
500–1,000	Tenn., Mont.
1,001–1,499	Mich., Kans., Mo., W.Va.
1,500–1,999	Minn., N.Dak., Ky.
Over 2,000	Wis., Iowa, Nebr., S.Dak.

SOURCE: *School Life* 42 (Feb. 1960): 13.

resistance to the destruction of their schools in the early 1950s. Reporting on "Schools without Students" in Nebraska in 1953, *Time* magazine found two hundred schools without students that were still being maintained. The article summed up the reason in the words of a Holt County rancher: "My grandpa learned in that there school. So did I, and so did my kids. If I got anything to say about it, my kids' kids will be learning in that self-same little school."

Those like him, who refused to accept the passing of their one-room schools—and there were many—found ways to impede the progress of consolidation. In some counties, they simply refused to select a county committee to plan the reorganization; in others, the committees met once, then decided to do nothing. Some county committees drew plans consolidating schools in only part of the county, thereby violating at least the spirit of the law. Finally, in many places, farmers simply refused to approve the reorganization after it had been completed, which was, of course, their right.

How hard it was for midwestern farmers to give up their little schools was disclosed in the statistics. In thirty-seven of the forty-eight states in 1958, the number of one-roomers ranged from fewer than ten to one thousand. But seven midwestern states had more than a thousand, and four had more than two thousand. [Table 11.2]

In that year, only slightly more than 25,000 one-room schoolhouses out of a total of 196,037 were left nationwide, and the vast majority were in the Midwest.

A few one-room schools here and there escaped the consolidation network, until finally there were no more students and no prospects of more. In many places in the rural Midwest, consolidation came not because the farmers necessarily believed that larger schools were better but simply because their districts ran out of children. The farmers in District No. 17 in York County, Nebraska, had maintained their school for years for only a handful of students. But in May 1955, when one of its two students graduated, the school board reluctantly closed the school. At the end of the school term, the graduate, the one remaining student, the teacher, and a young visitor pledged allegiance for the last time in the school's one room. [Illus. 11.9]

More soul-searching was needed to close the Pleasant Prairie School in Webster County, Nebraska. This ninety-six-year-old school, immortalized in "The Best Years," Willa Cather's story of a heroic fifteen-year-old teacher, still had seven students enrolled in 1970. Like so many country schools, it was the community center. It had once served as a church, and pioneers who had helped to build the community lay buried nearby. [Illus. 11.10] Nevertheless, in June of

11.9. *In 1955, only two students—one of whom was graduating—were enrolled in District No. 17, York County, Nebraska. This photograph captured the teacher, the two students, and a young visitor saying the Pledge of Allegiance for the last time before the school was closed. (Life, June 6, 1955, p. 61)*

that year, the decision was made to close the school and send the children into Red Cloud for schooling. The resolution had not come easily, and the agony of it reached all the way to the *Wall Street Journal*, which reported the story of the school's closing. But in the end, the educators won the argument. The majority of parents agreed that their children needed the competition of more of their peers to be successful.

But this acquiescence appeared to be the exception, not the rule. In Nebraska especially, and in other midwestern states as well, the closing of one-room schools came grudgingly one by one, not en masse countywide as the reorganization laws had intended. Nearly ten years after Nebraska's reorganization law had passed, the state still had 3,789 one-room schoolhouses (see Table 11.1). A few continued on into the 1980s, as did some in other midwestern states.

By then, country children had been passing through the doors of the small schoolhouse at Ellis Corner in Jackson County, Michigan, for more than a century. They had played beneath the school yard's shady trees and had, perhaps, attended the Methodist church across the road or visited the nearby store. [Illus. 11.11] But in 1987, almost no children were left in the district, and voters there had little choice but to close the school. At the end of that summer, it was carefully boarded up in the expectation that it would

11.11. For more than a century, children had played beneath the shade trees in this school yard and had, perhaps, attended the church across the way and visited the nearby store. Ellis Corner, Jackson County, Michigan.

11.10. Seven students were still enrolled in the Pleasant Prairie School—the setting for Willa Cather's story "The Best Years"—when the farmers decided to close it and send their children to school in Red Cloud. (Omaha World-Herald, *May 17, 1970)*

reopen when the district had three or four more children. [Illus. 11.12]

Although the little Ellis Corner School was able to withstand the pressures of consolidation until 1987, most of the Midwest's one-room schools faded away in the 1950s. In county after county, year after year, they were constantly being closed, and the few remaining children were bused to schools that were larger if not better. In most places, the small schools passed quietly from the scene to make way for progress. But here and there, the closing of the one-room schools was accompanied by a certain sadness among the farmers and their wives, as memories of the little schools flooded in upon them. In their youth, the one-room schools had been their

11.12. With almost no children left in the district, the Ellis Corner School was closed in 1986. Its windows were boarded up for protection, with the expectation that when the district had enough children it would reopen. Ellis Corner School, Jackson County, Michigan.

training ground for life and the remembered sites of their children's performances and last-day picnics. In those schools, the community had gathered, and it was obvious to them that closing their schools meant the eventual loss of their communities. So when it became known that a certain school would close, the last-day picnic became a special occasion, often attended by the oldest and youngest members of the district. Fried chicken, potato salad, and pies decorated the tables, and oldsters gathered to share golden memories and to reflect on what the little school had meant to them.

Perhaps not many thought of the closing of their school as the end of an era in the nation's history of education; nor is it likely that they speculated much about the nature of education in the big consolidated schools. Many had probably been convinced by years of arguments and the blandishments offered in reorganization campaigns that the big new schools would provide a better education for their children than the one they had received in the one-roomers. In any event, they accepted the inevitable and, at long last, left their little one-room schoolhouses to whatever fate awaited them.

Afterword

A.1. *When the last picnic was over and the doors were closed for the last time, some of the one-room schoolhouses were moved to town to be used until a larger schoolhouse could be built. (SHSI, Iowa City)*

When the last school picnic had been held and the schoolhouse door closed for the last time, the story of midwestern one-room schools was not quite finished. The question of what to do with the schoolhouse remained. Was it to be torn down, given away, sold, or left to rot where it stood? The answer was all of the above. At least a few were moved to town to serve as temporary schoolrooms until new schoolhouses could be built to accommodate the country children being bused into consolidated schools. In Sioux County, Iowa, some six of the old schools were crowded into town for this purpose. [Illus. A.1]

But mostly the little schools were sold at auction. In this process the first step was an advertisement in the local county paper. "Public Sale of School Houses" became a familiar announcement in county weeklies in the late forties and early fifties. In just this way the Ise schoolhouse (see chapters 3 and 6) came under the auctioneer's gavel. This old school, District No. 37, in Osborne County, Kansas, not far from the village of Downs and across the field from the Ise homestead, had been standing for sixty years when the Downs *News* announced that it and four others

A.2. *Most of the mid-*
western country
schools—like the Ise
School in District No.
37, Osborne County,
Kansas—were auc-
tioned off. (Downs,
Kans., News, *June 30,*
1946, p. 4)

would be auctioned off July 26, 1946. The sale price was not recorded. [Illus. A.2]

At most auctions more was offered for sale than the schoolhouse. On the day of the sale farmers gathered in the schoolyard to buy the school's contents as well. When the schoolhouse in District No. 39, Thayer County, Nebraska, was sold in 1949, farmers bought books and desks and swings, which together with the schoolhouse itself brought $1,110.31. Once the auction was over those who had lived within reach of their one-room school all their lives had only their memories left, "perhaps a billion dollars' worth," according to the *World-Herald* reporter. [Illus. A.3]

Such memories as they had were sometimes shared with one another when the auction of the schoolhouse served to reunite its former students. Men and women who had attended the Bush School, District No. 8, Plymouth Township, in Rock County, Wisconsin, had such a reunion in 1955. Their schoolhouse had been built in 1868, and though no larger than twenty by twenty-three feet, it had once accommodated ninety-three students. This number had been reduced to ten when it closed in 1947. In September, eight years later, it was sold at an auction at which former students reminisced. They saw for the last time the desks on which their names were carved and the corner of the room where they had been forced to stand for misbehavior. [Illus. A.4]

Like the schoolhouse in District No. 39, Thayer County, Nebraska, the Bush schoolhouse was purchased to be made into a home, and this was the fate of many of the Midwest's one-roomers.

Literally hundreds of them were remodeled into neat, attractive residences to serve the needs of families as they once had served to educate children. Driving along midwestern country roads today you may see a home immediately recognizable as a one-time country school. A changed front door, perhaps, or the addition of a porch is not enough to alter the signs of its former purpose. Some owners, indeed, deliberately retained certain schoolhouse features. With its window arrangement unchanged and belfry left intact, no one could mistake the Michigan home shown in Illus. A.5 for anything but a made-over country schoolhouse.

But others are not so obvious. Sometimes the only way to tell is to ask. Often only the occupants of a house standing where the old county plat indicates a school once stood can say whether their home was formerly a schoolhouse. A stranger would hardly know without asking, for example, that the house in Illus. A.6 (top) was once the schoolhouse for District No. 8, Elba Township, Dodge County, Wisconsin. (For the location of this former schoolhouse see section 32 on map, Illus. 1.4.)

On the other hand, the old iron pump in the foreground of the house in Illus. A.6 (bottom) might suggest that this was once a schoolyard,

A.3. *At auctions of country schools, farmers gathered in the school yard to buy the books, maps, globes, and desks that they and their children had once used. District No. 39, Thayer County, Nebraska. (Omaha* World-Herald, *Sept. 15, 1955, p. 4)*

but the house itself does not easily disclose its secret. Actually this was the Sanford School, District No. 5, in Woodstock Township, Lenawee County, Michigan, built in 1884 (see chapter 3). Likewise, only those who had lived in the neighborhood a long time would know that the stone and frame house with its huge chimney pictured in Illus. A.7 had been the Stone School, Joint District No. 8, Marcellon and Buffalo Townships, in Columbia County, Wisconsin. Built about 1867, it was a vital part of a thriving community that included a Baptist Church and cemetery and, a short distance away, a grist mill, built in 1887. Today only the Baptist Church remains active. The mill is silent save for the water from the mill pond spilling over the dam. Like the remodeled Stone Schoolhouse, they are now primarily points of historic interest for those who like to visualize what rural life was like in years gone by when children swarmed in the country schoolyard and farmers from miles around brought their grain there to be ground.

As often as not, however, the county plats of the 1880s or 1890s lead to a place where virtually nothing remains to mark the spot where a one-room schoolhouse once stood. Cows now graze where children, under the direction of a vigorous teacher, planted trees, fashioned an arbor in their schoolyard, and called their school

A.5. *Hundreds of one-room schoolhouses in the Midwest were made into homes. Some, like this one in Michigan, are clearly recognizable as former schoolhouses.*

the "Arbor Vitae School." Only parts of a foundation, invisible from the road, and a few trees remain to mark the site of that busy schoolhouse. [Illus. A.8; and see Illus. 5.22–5.24] The same is true of the much-publicized Porter School, District No. 3, in Adair County, Missouri. Not a board, not a stump, nor any of the school's outbuildings are left to mark the site. [Illus. A.9; and see Illus. 9.34–9.37]

What happened to schoolhouses like these? If they were not destroyed, they might have been moved to another location to become a granary, a house, or some other useful building. Some became community centers. One, not far from the town of Pratt in Pratt County, Kansas, is now the Richland Community Center. Another, near Chilicothe, Missouri, just off highway 65 in Livingston County, is the Liberty 4-H club meeting house. [Illus. A.10]

But many more have been left to decay. Frequently used by the farmers who purchased them for storage for a time, they have gone unrepaired and unpainted over the years until they are nearly beyond repair. This has been the melancholy fate of the Porter School, which drew so much national attention for its part in the revival of a rural community during the rural renaissance (see chapter 9). It was moved to a farmer's field some distance away, where it was used as a storehouse and over the years left to weather away. A makeshift door has replaced the original, a window has been broken, and even

Bush School Auction Is Reunion of Former Pupils

By MRS. RUTH MARTIN

When the Bush School, a mile south of Footville, went on the auction block Sept. 10 the event served as a reunion for pupils of up to half a century ago. Mark Walton, a former pupil, bought the school for $1,700 and plans to remodel it into a dwelling which he will rent; Emmett Murphy, register of deeds, returned to his alma mater to buy the maps of Rock County and the world, some dating back 60 years or more. Others purchased some of the other school furnishings while still others returned to see for the last time the spot where they had carved their initials, or the corner where they stood when the paper was delivered across the room land-ed on teacher's desk.

District 8 of Plymouth dates back to May 16, 1868, when the first school meeting was held in the Stephen Honeysette home, a meeting at which Samuel Honeysette served as chairman and was elected treasurer. James Hastings was the first clerk and Jeremiah Kinna, director.

A.4. *In some places, the auction of a schoolhouse served as a reunion for those who had once attended the school. (Janesville, Wis., Gazette, Sept. 15, 1955, p. 4)*

A.6. *Without asking their owners, it is impossible to tell that these country homes were once one-room schoolhouses. The top house was once the schoolhouse for District No. 8, Elba Township, Dodge County, Wisconsin. The house below was the schoolhouse for District No. 5, Woodstock Township, Lenawee County, Michigan.*

the hooks where children once hung their wraps have been broken off. [Illus. A.11]

This is also the story of the Ise Schoolhouse, so memorable a part of the community life described by John Ise in his book *Sod and Stubble*. Auctioned off in 1946, it was apparently never moved from its original site across the field from the Ise homestead. Photographed in the early

A.7. *The front part of the home pictured at the top was once the Stone School of Joint District No. 8, Marcellon and Buffalo Townships, Columbia County, Wisconsin. Close by are the cemetery, the Baptist church (middle), the mill, and the mill pond (bottom) that served the little community.*

1970s, it appeared in remarkably good condition considering the years of neglect. But time has been unkind. Uncared for through the years, it has deteriorated badly until in the late 1980s, with its windows broken and roof decaying, it seemed almost beyond any hope of restoration. [Illus. A.12]

And this has been the fate of so many country schoolhouses. Some wear better than others, of course. The Nebraska brick schoolhouse along highway 75 near the Otoe County line, boarded up and lonely looking, appears to be one of those ready to reopen should enough children make it feasible. By contrast, the Laurel Hill School, Dis-

A.10. Some one-room schoolhouses have been used for other public services. The schoolhouse pictured at the top, located not far from Pratt, Kansas, is now the Richland Community Center. The schoolhouse shown at the bottom, located in Livingston County, Missouri, is the Liberty 4-H club meeting house.

A.8. Cows graze where the Arbor Vitae School, Subdistrict No. 7, Oneida Township, Delaware County, Iowa, once stood.

A.9. Nothing remains in this field to suggest that this was the location of the famous Porter School in District No. 3, Adair County, Missouri.

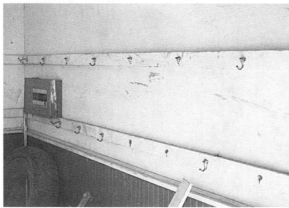

A.11. *The Porter School in District No. 3, Adair County, Missouri, was moved to a farmer's field some distance from its original site. There it was used as a storehouse and left largely uncared for.*

trict No. 48 in Clay County, Kansas, on highway 24 shows the toll neglect has taken. [Illus. A.13]

Happily a number of the old buildings have been preserved as museums. It is unfortunate that so many have been displayed simply as quaint pioneer schoolhouses and so few as the main-stays of the rural Midwest's educational system in which, as recently as World War II, thousands of country children received an education that was, arguably at least, comparable to that given many urban children today. But however these schools are presented, midwesterners proudly preserve them as symbols of their people's struggle to educate their children in the midst of adversity.

A few of the old schoolhouses have been preserved at their original sites. The Freeman School, District No. 21, in Gage County, near Beatrice, Nebraska, where so much trouble once occurred over the reading of the Bible (see chapter 6), has been renovated where it had always stood. Today it is a part of the Homestead National Monument and open to visitors in the summer. [Illus. A.14] Similarly, the Board of Education in Sedalia, Missouri, restored the McVey School near the site where it had served the children of Pettis County from 1883 to 1956. Fittingly, the project was dedicated to "all Teachers, Living and Deceased." [Illus. A.15]

Above and right: A.12. *The Ise School in District No. 37, Osborne County, Kansas, remains on its original site. But its steady deterioration from the early 1970s (above) to the late 1980s (right) is reflected in these pictures.*

A number of old one-roomers have been moved from their original sites to college campuses across the region. There, at schools which were once normals (teacher-training schools), then teachers' colleges, and now universities, they are useful tools for instruction in the history of education. The College of the Ozarks, in southwestern Missouri, is only one of many such schools of higher education to preserve a country school. In 1972 it brought the old Star School, District No. 38, Barry County, from its place near McDowell to its campus, where it is now a part of the Ralph Foster museum. [Illus. A.16]

Sometimes an old country schoolhouse has been preserved because of its connection with an

A.14. *Fortunately, some midwestern country schoolhouses have been preserved in museums of one kind or another. This schoolhouse from District No. 21, Gage County, Nebraska, is part of the Homestead National Monument near Beatrice, Nebraska, and is open to visitors.*

A.15. *The preservation of the McVey School in Pettis County, Missouri, has been dedicated to teachers.*

A.13. *Some abandoned one-room schoolhouses have held up better than others. With its windows boarded up, the brick schoolhouse located on Highway 75 near the Otoe County line in Nebraska (top) appears ready to reopen if necessary. Less care has been taken of the schoolhouse that once served District No. 48 in Clay County, Kansas (bottom).*

illustrious citizen. For just this reason the citizens of Grundy Center, a small town in Grundy County, Iowa, of fewer than three thousand people, have preserved the Herbert Quick Schoolhouse (see chapter 6). This old building was hauled into town from the country where one of the county's most illustrious citizens had attended it and was made into a museum of pioneer education. Teacher, lawyer, and novelist, Herbert Quick, remarking on the dread he felt on his first day in this school in *One Man's Life*, paid tribute to his education there. "The teacher, a kind coun-

A.16. *Small midwestern universities—formerly normal schools and teachers' colleges—have preserved country schoolhouses on their campuses, where they continue to serve education. Star School, District No. 85, Barry County, Missouri. (Ralph Foster Museum, Ozark College, Point Lookout, Mo.)*

A.18. *One-room school preservations—usually displayed as pioneer institutions—rarely reflect the fact that they were at the heart of the Midwest's system of rural education until after World War II. Country children were educated in this schoolhouse, now at the Museum of Prairie Living in Colby, Kansas, until 1943.*

try girl, came and comforted me, took my name and age, and was surprised because I had been through the Fifth Reader time and again, and had a big geography. Soon, of course, I was an intimate in the little society and as happy as any schoolboy. And in this schoolhouse I was to receive all the formal schooling I was ever to have." [Illus. A.17]

Colby, a western Kansas town of fewer than

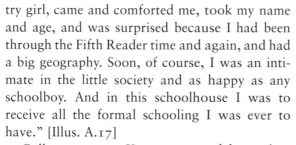

A.17. *The citizens of Grundy County, Iowa, have preserved the Herbert Quick School in Grundy Center. Herbert Quick, one of the county's most illustrious citizens, received all his formal education here. (SHSI, Iowa City)*

six thousand people, has a museum not merely of pioneer life but of Prairie Living, where the Nicol Schoolhouse, District No. 15 in Thomas County, Kansas, is appropriately displayed. Children first went to this school in 1887. In 1931, like others of its kind, it was closed for lack of students. Reopened briefly in 1943 for four students, it was closed again, used as a voting precinct for a time, and in 1949 became a Home Demonstration building before it was moved to the museum. [Illus. A.18]

Like most midwestern states, Kansas has a number of such restorations, and some are still used for educational purposes. On grounds that more realistically resemble a schoolyard than many preservations have available, the Kansas State Historical Society in Topeka has restored a one-room schoolhouse complete with bell, belfry, pump, and flagpole. It is equipped so that visiting children may have classes there. [Illus. A.19]

But the State Historical Society's preservation is no more impressive than the country schoolhouse restoration in Lindsborg, Kansas. Set in Heritage Square in the McPherson County Old Mill and Park complex, this one-room schoolhouse was built in 1903, used until 1952, and brought to the site in 1967. [Illus. A.20] With its interior arranged much as it was when last used in 1952 and equipped with old spellers, readers,

A.19. *On the ample grounds of its museum in To-peka, the Kansas State Historical Society has pre-served this one-room schoolhouse and made it available for classes of elementary school children.*

A.21. *The interior of the West Kentuck Schoolhouse in Heritage Square is arranged much as it was in 1952, when it was closed. Students are bused from around the region to this schoolhouse, and classes are held in it almost daily during the week.*

A.20. *Among the numerous preservations that make up the McPherson County, Kansas, Old Mill and Park complex in Lindsborg is this country school-house placed in the complex's Heritage Square.*

and maps, West Kentuck School, as it was named, is now used to link the area's children with their heritage. Almost daily during the school year children from around the area are bused to this school, where their teachers hold regular classes. [Illus. A.21]

One day in that small classroom is not enough, of course, to teach young children all the lessons to be derived from the one-room school experience. So different was that world from theirs it is unlikely that in so short a time they can be made to fully understand that a small school can be a good school; that parents were once intimately involved in the schooling of their children; that money alone cannot buy a good education; that neither a fine building nor a proliferation of teaching aids is necessary for learning; that the three R's really are basic; that drills can be helpful learning tools; that memorization can serve as the handmaiden to thinking; and that testing students need not be harmful.

Still, sitting in that small room with the past sweeping in upon them, they will perhaps learn to appreciate their own comfortable classrooms and be inspired to take advantage of the bounteous opportunities they have to further their education and to be whatever they wish to be. This, at least, could be their legacy from the one-room schools of their ancestors.

Index